PRACTISE
MENTAL
MATHS

for ages
10-11

PRACTISE MENTAL MATHS for ages 10-11

Introduction

Practise Mental Maths is a carefully planned series of quick daily mental maths tests that are structured to improve children's numeracy skills. In each book there are 190 tests – one for every day of the school year. The series is closely matched to the Numeracy Framework and has been devised to help develop pupils' numeracy skills in fun short bursts!

The tests get progressively more difficult as you work through the book so that children can gradually improve their speed and accuracy. All the tests follow the same structure of ten questions spilt into three sections: **Warm up**, **Quick fire** and **Problem solver**. A small working out space is provided for the **Problem solver** question but remember to have extra scrap paper available for children who need it.

If you would prefer not to read out the test questions yourself, use the accompanying CD-ROM. In this way pupils can work independently. You might like to use the tests at the beginning or end of the day, or at those times when you have a spare five minutes to fill. All the pages are provided as PDFs for you to display on a white board or print out as individual sheets. For quick and easy checking answers are included at the back of the book.

The accompanying CD-ROM contains mp3 audio files of all the tests that can be played on music systems that are MP3 compatible and computers with itunes or windows media player. (Please note that the CDs do not operate on ordinary CD players. For full operating instructions see the inside cover of this book.) Each question is read out twice and there is a 10 second gap between each question.

Test 1

Warm up

1. Double 97.

2. How many 50p coins are there in £100?

   200

3. 1500 + 300 + 60 = ? *1860*

Quick fire

4. What fraction is the shaded part?

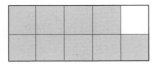

   9/10

5. What number is exactly halfway between 1100 and 1500?

6. 60 + 60 = ? *120*

7. 40 + 80 = ? *120*

8. 75 + 45 = ? *120*

9. 95 + 25 = ? *120*

Problem solver

10. 8,412 planes landed at the Wright Airport in 2010. This was an increase of 763 on the previous year. How many planes landed at the airport in 2009?

Test 2

Warm up

1. Draw a parallelogram.

2. Circle the number which is not an exact multiple of 6.

   36 18 39 48 72

3. What time would it be 1 hour 10 minutes before 9:05?

Quick fire

4. Find the difference between 5420 and 6820.

5. Order these numbers, starting with the smallest.

   5794   4876   4902   6381   7002

   ___ ___ ___ ___ ___

6. 150 – 50 = ? _____

7. 195 – 95 = ? _____

8. 200 – 100 = ?_____

9. 105 – 5 = ? _____

Problem solver

10. 7,416 visitors came to the Estuary Bird Sanctuary last year. 9,492 people have booked for this year. What is the total numbers of visitors over the two years?

Name ....

Name ....

Practise Mental Maths 10 – 11 ©A&C Black 2011

Test 3

1. Double 147. _____

2. Circle the number that is closest to 5000.

5050   4994   5100   5500   4500

3. Circle the number which is not exactly divisible by 7.

70   21   49   77   67

Quick fire

4. Round these numbers to the nearest 1000.

31047   33154   22807   49711   65828

_____ _____ _____ _____ _____

5. Which number is half way between

1150 and 1500? _____

1870 and 2870? _____

6. $10 \times 9 = ?$ _____

7. $12 \times 9 = ?$ _____

8. $13 \times 9 = ?$ _____

9. $11 \times 9 = ?$ _____

Problem solver

10. The Jones family have driven 4,926 miles this year, visiting all their relatives, and 6,734 miles on a touring holiday of Europe. How far have they travelled this year?

_____

Test 4

1. Write a pair of numbers which total 1000.

_____ + _____ = 1000

2. Multiply each of these numbers by 2

22 _____   46 _____   100 _____

3. $462 - ? = 100$ _____

Quick fire

4. Round these fractions to the nearest whole number.

$242\frac{1}{10}$ _____ $17\frac{9}{16}$ _____ $36\frac{8}{12}$ _____

5. Circle the smaller number in each pair.

5131   5927   5974   5794

6. $0 \div 9 = ?$ _____

7. $18 \div 9 = ?$ _____

8. $27 \div 9 = ?$ _____

9. $9 \div 9 = ?$ _____

Problem solver

10. 376 children took their chairs to the field to watch Sports Day. Half of them put their chairs along the track. The rest put them at the finish. How many chairs were along the track?

_____

me ....   Name ....

Test 5

Warm up

1. What is half of 4560?

   _____

2. Write a subtraction problem where the answer is 324.

   _____ – _____ = 324

3. Add the digits in today's date.

   _____

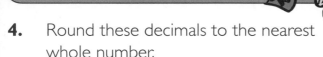

Quick fire

4. Round these decimals to the nearest whole number.

   502.441   828.352   6609.868   6437.667

   _____   _____   _____   _____

5. Estimate the numbers on this line.

   1g [ ] [ ] 20g

6. $108 + 103 + 105 = ?$ _____

7. $101 + 99 + 97 = ?$ _____

8. $101 + 91 + 11 = ?$ _____

9. $101 + 19 + 61 = ?$ _____

Problem solver

10. James and Kit were asked to count the books in the science and history sections of the school library. There were 476 science books and 834 history books. How many books were there altogether?

    _____

Name ....

Test 6

Warm up

1. Write this number in words: 6460.

   _____

   _____

2. Add 50 to each of these numbers.

   10 _____   20 _____   30 _____

3. What is the answer to this calculation chain?

   $3 + 1 + 2 \times 8 = ?$ _____

Quick fire

4. Circle the numbers which are exact multiples of 8.

   1469   200   2938   4488   5552

5. Underline the larger number in each pair.

   6829   6541   7001 7011

6. $191 - 91 - 19 = ?$ _____

7. $211 - 101 - 10 = ?$ _____

8. $157 - 131 - 17 = ?$ _____

9. $153 - 13 - 21 = ?$ _____

Problem solver

10. The city library lends 4076 books in July and 7932 books in August. How many more books did they lend in August?

    _____

Name ....

Practise Mental Maths 10 – 11 ©A&C Black 2011

Test 7

1. Circle the odd number.

416   522   6881   9222

2. Multiply each of these numbers by 3.

9 ____   6 ____   12 ____

3. How many minutes are there in 3.5 hours?

_____

Quick fire

4. Circle the numbers which are exactly divisible by 8.

6100   1608   1600   1060   1552

5. Underline the smaller number in each pair.

4826   4286   3917   3971

6. $5 \times 9 = ?$ _____

7. $6 \times 9 = ?$ _____

8. $4 \times 9 = ?$ _____

9. $7 \times 9 = ?$ _____

Problem solver

10. Mrs James, the school secretary, ordered 1000 pens on a special offer. By the end of the year, 639 of the pens were left. How many pens had been used?

_____

Name _____

Test 8

Warm up

1. Which number is 4002 more than 36?

_____

2. What time would it be 2 hours 50 minutes after 16:36?

3. What is 5% of £1? _____

Quick fire

4. Continue the sequence.

40   44 ____ ____ ____ ____ ____

5. Estimate the numbers on this line.

0 _____ 1.5m

6. $45 \div 9 = ?$ _____

7. $54 \div 9 = ?$ _____

8. $36 \div 9 = ?$ _____

9. $63 \div 9 = ?$ _____

Problem solver

10. Louis had 1097 red poppy seeds and 3427 yellow poppy seeds. How many more yellow seeds does Louis have?

_____

Name _____

Test 9

1. What is two thirds of 27?

   _____

2. $126 - 32 = ?$ _____

3. What is 5% of 1 metre? _____

Quick fire

4. Continue the sequence of 4, starting at 43 and stopping at 75.

   43 ___ ___ ___ ___ ___ ___ ___ 75

5. Order these decimals. Start with the smallest.

      .5   .89   .12   .32   .2

   ___ ___ ___ ___ ___

6. $100 + 60 = ?$ _____

7. $120 + 40 = ?$ _____

8. $80 + 80 = ?$ _____

9. $90 + 70 = ?$ _____

Problem solver

10. The train from London had 365 people on it. At Birmingham 38 people got off, and 46 got on. At Manchester 61 people got off, and 18 got on. How many people were on the train when it left Manchester?

    _____

Name _____

Test 10

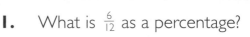

Warm up

1. What is $\frac{6}{12}$ as a percentage?

   _____

2. Write a multiplication problem where the answer is 18.

   _____ × _____ = 18

3. What time would it be 3 hours 30 minutes before 12:42?

Quick fire

4. Continue this sequence of fractions.

   $34\frac{1}{2}$ 35   ___ ___ ___ ___

5. Estimate the months on this timeline.

   Sept   [ ]   [ ]   May

6. $130 - 60 = ?$ _____

7. $190 - 120 = ?$ _____

8. $158 - 88 = ?$ _____

9. $150 - 80 = ?$ _____

Problem solver

10. Year 6 have 103 spellings for homework each month. Last month Brenda got all but 17 correct. What was her score?

    _____

Name _____

Test 11

Warm up

1. Write the number 5021 in words.

   _____

2. What do I add to 1000 to make 1111?

   _____

3. How many spots are there on 8 seven spot ladybirds?

   _____

Quick fire

4. Continue this sequence of decimals.

   30.3   30.4   _____   _____   _____

5. Write this division calculation as a multiplication calculation.

   150 ÷ 50 = 3   _____

6. ? × 9 = 36   _____

7. ? × 9 = 54   _____

8. ? × 9 = 27   _____

9. ? × 9 = 90   _____

Problem solver

10. Donna has 1534 game cards in her collection. She gives Fergus 112 cards, then Jan gives Donna 39 cards. How many does she have now?

    _____

Name ....

Test 12

Warm up

1. Write this number in figures: seventy three thousand five hundred and twelve.

   _____

2. Write a number between 5000 and 5500 that is nearer 5500.

   _____

3. What is 5% of 200? _____

Quick fire

4. Write this addition calculation as a subtraction calculation.

   76 + 53 = 129   _____

5. Estimate the numbers on this line.

6. ? ÷ 9 = 4   _____

7. ? ÷ 9 = 6   _____

8. ? ÷ 9 = 3   _____

9. ? ÷ 9 = 10   _____

Problem solver

10. A baby elephant weighs about 125 kilos at birth. By the time it is an adult it weighs 50 times as much. How much does an adult elephant weigh?

    _____

Name ....

Test 13

Warm up

1. Write a number between 3000 and 3017 that is nearer to 3017.

   _____

2. Circle the number which is half of 6000.

   600   3000   300

3. What is 25% of £4? _____

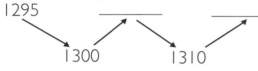

Quick fire

4. Find the missing numbers.

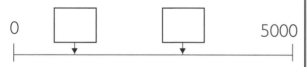

   1295   _____   _____

            1300   1310

5. Estimate the numbers on this line.

   0 [ ]   [ ]   5000

6. 80 + 80 + 80 = ? _____

7. 60 + 60 + 60 = ? _____

8. 40 + 40 + 40 = ? _____

9. 48 + 48 + 48 = ? _____

Problem solver

10. Missing number.
    If you divide this number by 5 and add 30 the answer will be 80. What is the missing number?

    _____

Test 14

Warm up

1. Round 6463 to the nearest 10.

   _____

2. Circle the number which is not an exact multiple of 7.

   35   51   42   28   56

3. What is 75% of £8? _____

Quick fire

4. Halve these numbers.

   256   848   1200   388

   _____   _____   _____   _____

5. What are the largest and smallest numbers you can make with these digits? 0   5   9   1   5

   Largest _____ Smallest _____

6. 210 – 110 – 40 = ? _____

7. 192 – 100 – 48 = ? _____

8. 160 – 124 – 14 = ? _____

9. 158 – 28 – 100 = ? _____

Problem solver

10. There are 45 chocolates in a box. 20% are mints. How many mint chocolates are there in a box?

    _____

Name ....

Name ....

Practise Mental Maths 10 – 11 ©A&C Black 2011

Test 15

Warm up

1. Round this decimal to the nearest integer or whole number: 67.38

   _____

2. What is half of 2.2?

   _____

3. Write a multiplication problem where the answer is 90.

   _____ × _____ = 90

Quick fire

4. Give the value in £ of

    × 60

   _____

5. Add these decimals.
   13.05 + 16.25 + 79.65 = _____

   Fill in the missing numbers in these sequences.

6. ____ ____ 17 11 5

7. ____ ____ 14 ____ 2

8. ____ ____ ____ 9 3

9. ____ ____ 16 ____ 4

Problem solver

10. The museum turnstile showed 6412 at mid-day and 8319 at closing time. How many visitors came to the museum during the afternoon?

    _____

Test 16

Warm up

1. What is half of 5000?

   _____

2. 480 ÷ 8 =

   _____

3. How many minutes are there in 12.5 hours?

   _____

Quick fire

4. Double these numbers.

   346   519   827   776

   _____   _____   _____   _____

5. What is the smallest decimal number you can make with these digits?
   1 2 8 4 7

   _____

6. (14 ÷ 2) × (21 ÷ 7) = ? _____

7. (54 ÷ 9) × (36 ÷ 6) = ? _____

8. (49 ÷ 7) × (48 ÷ 6) = ? _____

9. (63 ÷ 7) × (70 ÷ 10) =? _____

Problem solver

10. Sasha is 2 years younger than Julie. The sum of their ages is 96. How old are Sasha and Julie?

    _____

Name _____

Name _____

Test 17

Warm up

1. Divide each of these numbers by 10.

10   50   100

_____   _____   _____

2. Choose the correct operation for this calculation.

126 ____ 32 = 94

3. What time would it be 6 hours 10 minutes after 15:17?

Quick fire

4. What needs to be added to 1291 to make 3562?

_____

5. Estimate the decimal numbers on this line.

0 ———————————————— 1

6. 100 + 25 = ? _____

7. 75 + 50 = ? _____

8. 95 + 30 = ? _____

9. 90 + 36 = ? _____

Problem solver

10. John offered to put out the chairs for Sports Day. There were 7 rows of 11 chairs on each side of the track and 5 rows of 11 at each end. How many chairs did John put out?

_____

Name _____

Test 18

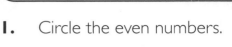

Warm up

1. Circle the even numbers.

619   844   723   852

2. Write an addition problem where the answer is 2176.

_____ + _____ = 2176

3. 24 ÷ 6 + 10 = _____

Quick fire

4. What needs to be subtracted from 749 to make 250?

_____

5. What is the total weight of

310g + 149g + 305g + 220g?

_____

6. 159 – 64 = ? _____

7. 151 – 56 = ? _____

8. 157 – 72 = ? _____

9. 153 – 58 = ? _____

Problem solver

10. Dean, the DJ played his favourite song at 9 o'clock each day on his morning radio show for 147 days. How many weeks is that?

_____

Name _____

Test 19

Warm up

1. Which number is 76 less than 100?

   _____

2. $7 \times 9 + 17 =$ _____

3. How many eyes on are there 90 snakes?

   _____

Quick fire

4. Continue the sequence of 4 starting at 86 and stopping at 110.

   86 ____ ____ ____ ____ ____ 110

5. What is the total weight of

   $180g + 140g + 430g + 335g?$ _____

6. $6 \times 9 =$ ___ $\times$ ___

7. $3 \times 9 =$ ___ $\times$ ___

8. $2 \times 9 =$ ___ $\times$ ___

9. ___ $\times 9 =$ ___ $\times 8$

Problem solver

10. Zoe had £74.93. Her uncle gave her £23.10. How much does she have now?

   _____

Test 20

Warm up

1. Which is less? 5 thousandths or 51 hundredths?

   _____

2. Add 60 to each of these numbers.

   5   15   30

   _____   _____   _____

3. $290 + 1500 + 70 = ?$ _____

Quick fire

4. Continue the sequence.

   38   45   ___ ___ ___ ___ ___ ___

5. What number is exactly halfway between 3870 and 5870?

   _____

6. $54 \div 6 = 45 \div ?$ _____

7. $72 \div 9 = 48 \div ?$ _____

8. $40 \div 8 = 35 \div ?$ _____

9. $81 \div 9 = 27 \div ?$ _____

Problem solver

10. Mystery Number.
    I am a number between 60 and 100.
    I can be divided exactly by 2 and 4.
    You say me when you count in 20s.

   _____

Name ....

Name ....

Test 21

Warm up

1. Double 126. _____

2. Write a number between 1050 and 2050 that is nearer 1050.

   _____

3. $81 - 9 + 20 = ?$ _____

Quick fire

4. What fraction is the shaded part?

   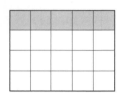

   _____

5. Continue this sequence of decimals.

   48.2 48.3 _____ _____ _____ _____

6. $100 + 10 = 20 + ?$ _____

7. $90 + 20 = 70 + ?$ _____

8. $80 + 30 = 60 + ?$ _____

9. $95 + 15 = 85 + ?$ _____

Problem solver

10. At Johnny's school $\frac{1}{2}$ of the children bought school lunch and $\frac{7}{20}$ of the children brought sandwiches. The rest of the children went home for lunch. What fraction of the children went home?

    _____

Name _____

Test 22

Warm up

1. Draw a kite.

2. Circle the numbers which are exact multiples of 8.

   32   45   48   36   88

3. $147 - 57 \div 9$ _____

Quick fire

4. Count on in steps of 0.5 from 1.

   1 _____ _____ _____ _____

5. Estimate the numbers on this line.

   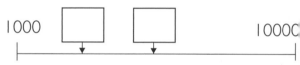

6. $100 - 10 = 190 - ?$ _____

7. $170 - 80 = 180 - ?$ _____

8. $150 - 60 = 200 - ?$ _____

9. $195 - 105 = 105 - ?$ _____

Problem solver

10. During the winter, the children at Woodbine School drank 2,649 gallons of water from the drinking fountain. During the summer they drank double this amount of water. How much did they drink during the summer?

    _____

Name _____

Test 23

Warm up

1. Circle the number nearest to 2500.

   2994   2436   2650   2369   2461

2. Write a subtraction problem where the answer is 891.

   _____ − _____ = 891

3. How many legs on 56 postmen?

   _____

Quick fire

4. Round these numbers to the nearest 1000.

   31409   33154   22807   71793   49711

   _____ _____ _____ _____ _____

5. Order these, starting with the smallest.

   45794 45876 44902 47002 46385

   _____ _____ _____ _____ _____

6. $110 \times 2 = ?$ _____

7. $222 \times 2 = ?$ _____

8. $250 \times 2 = ?$ _____

9. $330 \times 2 = ?$ _____

Problem solver

10. Tim, the trainee tea bag maker, made 38,704 tea bags. 9,295 bags were substandard. How many tea bags went on to be packed?

    _____

Test 24

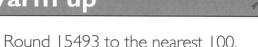

Warm up

1. Round 15493 to the nearest 100.

   _____

2. Multiply 150 by 5.

   _____

3. Add 28 to each of these numbers 2.

   7   14   21

   _____   _____   _____

Quick fire

4. Round these fractions to the nearest whole number.

   $12\frac{24}{100}$ ____ $16\frac{62}{90}$ ____ $9\frac{84}{500}$ ____

5. Underline the smaller number in each pair.

   9001   9010   8575   8775

6. $220 \div 2 = ?$ _____

7. $444 \div 2 = ?$ _____

8. $500 \div 2 = ?$ _____

9. $650 \div 2 = ?$ _____

Problem solver

10. Parvinder was packing up the library books for the holidays. She put 20 books in each box and she packed 25 boxes. How many books did she pack?

    _____

Name ....

Name ....

Test 25

Warm up

1. What is half of 5500?

   _____

2. Divide each of these numbers by 9.

      27   45   72

   _____   _____   _____

3. How many minutes are there in 14 hours 55 minutes?

   _____

Quick fire

4. Round these decimals to the nearest whole number.

   1632.231   6776.677   4932.169   7121.852

   _____   _____   _____   _____

5. Estimate the measures on this line.

   50g [   ]   [   ]   100g

6. $195 + 5 = ?$ _____

7. $95 + 105 = ?$ _____

8. $75 + 125 = ?$ _____

9. $55 + 145 = ?$ _____

Problem solver

10. 8 CDs fit in a CD case. Sunil has 56 CDs. How many cases does he need to hold his collection of CDs?

    _____

Name _____

Test 26

Warm up

1. Write this number in words: 80300

   _____

   _____

2. What is the answer to this calculation chain?

   $373 - 173 \times 2 = ?$ _____

3. What is 75% of 1000? _____

Quick fire

4. Circle the numbers which are exact multiples of 9.

   4299   8164   25   5418   3313

5. Underline the smaller number in each pair.

   9323   9129   7346   7461

6. $115 - 35 = ?$ _____

7. $101 - 21 = ?$ _____

8. $117 - 37 = ?$ _____

9. $105 - 25 = ?$ _____

Problem solver

10. Garry bought a football for £24.80, a new pair of football socks for £2.99 and a Rover's ruler for 99p. How much did he spend altogether?

    _____

Name _____

Test 27

1. Circle the number which is half of 7000.

530   3500   350

2. Write a multiplication problem where the answer is 64.

_____ × _____ = 64

3. What time would it be 1 hour 16 minutes before 12:36?

4. Circle the numbers which are exactly divisible by 12.

3131   2121   3636   2424   6060

5. Estimate the numbers on this line.

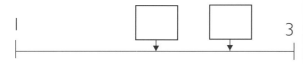

1   3

6. 115 × 2 = ? _____

7. 211 × 2 = ? _____

8. 207 × 2 = ? _____

9. 199 × 2 = ? _____

10. Martina cycles to her new school every day, a distance of 76 miles each week. This is twice as far as she cycled to her old school. How far did she cycle to her old school each week?

_____

Name _____

Test 28

1. Circle the even numbers.

1793   1847   1226   208

2. How many corners are there on 39 hexagons?

_____

3. What is 25% of 1kg?

_____

4. Continue the sequence.

112   118   124 ____ ____ ____ ____

5. Estimate the measures on this line.

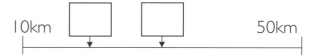

10km   50km

6. 230 ÷ 2 = ? _____

7. 422 ÷ 2 = ? _____

8. 414 ÷ 2 = ? _____

9. 398 ÷ 2 = ? _____

10. Robert read a 135 page book in January and a book with twice as many pages in February. How long was the book he read in February?

_____

Name _____

Test 29

Warm up

1. What is 1210 more than 2210?

   _____

2. Write a pair of numbers which total 7002.

   _____ + _____ = 7002

3. 329 + ? = 500

   _____

Quick fire

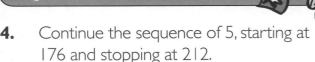

4. Continue the sequence of 5, starting at 176 and stopping at 212.

   176 ____ ____ ____ ____ ____ 212

5. Order these decimals. Start with the smallest.

   5.3   5.63   5.9   5.36   5.09

   ____ ____ ____ ____ ____

6. 100 + 100 = ? _____

7. 80 + 120 = ? _____

8. 86 + 114 = ? _____

9. 90 + 120 = ? _____

Problem solver

10. Mark bought 576 football cards from a sale. He gave half to Sam and 20 to his brother. How many cards did Mark have left?

    _____

Name _____

Test 30

Warm up

1. What is three ninths of 36?

   _____

2. Which is less? 59 hundreds or 6 thousands?

   _____

3. What is 10% of £20? _____

Quick fire

4. Continue this sequence of fractions.

   $19\frac{1}{2}$ $19\frac{3}{4}$ ____ ____ ____ ____

5. Estimate the dates on this line.

   31 Oct [____][____] 31 Dec

6. 120 − 12 = 118 − ? _____

7. 116 − 24 = 112 − ? _____

8. 100 − 20 = 120 − ? _____

9. 118 − 18 = 120 − ? _____

Problem solver

10. A farmer is planting potatoes. He has 50 sacks, each containing 100 potatoes. He plants half before it gets too dark to see. How many potatoes are left to plant the next day?

    _____

Name _____

Practise Mental Maths 10 – 11 ©A&C Black 2011

Test 31

Warm up

1. Round 4345 to the nearest ten.

   _____

2. How many £2 coins can you make out of £466?

   _____

3. What is 75% of 1 litre?

   _____

Quick fire

4. What needs to be subtracted from 8319 to make 4022?

   _____

5. Write this multiplication calculation as a division calculation.

   $15 \times 4 = 60$ _____

6. $(2 \times 9) + (4 \times 9) = ?$ _____

7. $(1 \times 9) + (7 \times 9) = ?$ _____

8. $(9 \times 9) - (3 \times 9) = ?$ _____

9. $(10 \times 9) - (2 \times 9) = ?$ _____

Problem solver

10. Jinny and Jenny, the twins, want new bikes for their birthday. The bikes cost £180.97 each. How much will their parents have to pay for the two bikes?

    _____

Name ....

Test 32

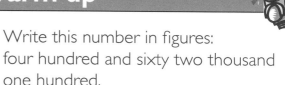

Warm up

1. Write this number in figures: four hundred and sixty two thousand one hundred.

   _____

2. Circle the number which is not an exact multiple of 9.

   26   18   99   27   36

3. How many nails are there on 30 hands?

   _____

Quick fire

4. Find the difference between 710 and 6711.

   _____

5. Complete this addition calculation and write it as a subtraction calculation.

   $553 + 448 =$ ____ ____ − ____ = ____

6. $(54 \div 9) \div 2 = ?$ _____

7. $(72 \div 9) \div 2 = ?$ _____

8. $(81 \div 9) \div 2 = ?$ _____

9. $(90 \div 9) \div 2 = ?$ _____

Problem solver

10. Leanne went shopping with her auntie. They left home at 8.45am and returned at 6.20pm. How long were they away?

    _____

Name ....

Test 33

1. Write a number between 3600 and 4800 that is nearer to 4800.

   _____

2. Multiply 17 by 6. _____

3. What time would it be 95 minutes after 10:42?

Quick fire

4. Fill in the missing numbers.

   1962   2062   2162

   _____   _____

5. Estimate the numbers on this line.

   -20   [ ]   [ ]   20

6. $86 + 90 + 86 = ?$ _____

7. $84 + 86 + 96 = ?$ _____

8. $97 + 93 + 80 = ?$ _____

9. $96 + 88 + 90 = ?$ _____

Problem solver

10. On games day at school $\frac{8}{21}$ of the class wanted to play rounders, $\frac{1}{3}$ of the class wanted to play football and the rest wanted to play cricket. What fraction wanted to play cricket?

    _____

Name ....

Test 34

Warm up

1. Round this decimal to the nearest integer or whole number: 67.370

   _____

2. What is half of 5005?

   _____

3. Write a pair of numbers which total 3156.

   _____ + _____ = 3156

Quick fire

4. Halve these numbers.

   530   984   2085   1509

   _____ _____ _____ _____

5. What are the largest and smallest numbers you can make with these digits? 1   2   8   4   7

   Largest _____ Smallest _____

6. $200 - 80 = ?$ _____

7. $180 - 60 = ?$ _____

8. $140 - 20 = ?$ _____

9. $160 - 50 = ?$ _____

Problem solver

10. George is helping his mum to make a new path in his grandma's garden. The garden is 16.25m long. Paving slabs are 1.25m long. How many slabs do they need for the path?

    _____

Name ....

Test 35

1. What is half of 10.5?

_____

2. Write a multiplication problem where the answer is 63.

_____ × _____ = 63

3. Subtract 50 from each of these numbers.

    60   70   80

_____ _____ _____

Quick fire

4. Give the value in £ of × 102

_____

5. What is the total weight of 550g + 650g + 250g + 750g?

_____

6. 15 × 9 = (10 × ___) + (5 × ___)

7. 20 × 9= (___ × ___) + (10 × 9)

8. 18 × 9 = (10 × ___) + (___ × ___)

9. 17 × 9= (10 × ___) + (7 × ___)

Problem solver

10. There are 180 drawing pins in a box. 25% of them are red. How many red pins are there in 5 boxes?

_____

Test 36

Warm up

1. Write the number which is half of 7050.

_____

2. Add 25 to each of these numbers.

    50   70   90

_____ _____ _____

3. 11 × 6 ÷ 12 = ?

_____

Quick fire

4. Double these numbers.

  192   287   856   5410

_____ _____ _____ _____

5. What is the smallest decimal number you can make with these digits?

0 9 9 7 8 0 _____

6. 81 ÷ 9 = half of ? _____

7. 72 ÷ ? = half of 16 _____

8. 56 ÷ 8 = half of ? _____

9. 48 ÷ ? = half of 12 _____

Problem solver

10. Imagine a 0–99 number square. Which numbers are diagonally to the left of 67?

_____

Name ....

Test 37

Warm up

1. Circle the odd numbers.

   113   4142   9890   3413

2. Multiply each of these numbers by 5.

   4   14   11

   _____   _____   _____

3. How many minutes are there in 10 hours 49 minutes?

   _____

Quick fire

4. What needs to be added to 7645 to make 7841?

   _____

5. What is the total weight of

   150g + 150g + 510g + 950g? =

   _____

6. 200 + 50 = 100 + ? _____

7. 160 + 90 = 210 + ? _____

8. 190 + 60 = 240 + ? _____

9. 170 + 80 = 130 + ? _____

Problem solver

10. Andy is 21 years older than Kim. 7 years from now, Kim will be 25. How old is Andy now?

    _____

Name _____

Test 38

Warm up

1. Which number is 180 less than 1000?

   _____

2. 100 + 96 − 65 = ? _____

3. What is 25% of 4 hours?

   _____

Quick fire

4. Estimate the answer to the nearest 100.

   100 + 96 − 65

   _____

5. Add these decimals.

   15.14 + 25.20 + 32.88 =

   _____

6. (150 − 50) − 24 = ? _____

7. (180 − 55) − 45 = ? _____

8. (174 − 54) − 30 = ? _____

9. (177 − 39) − 33 = ? _____

Problem solver

10. Anna is half Paul's age. 6 years ago, Paul was 12. How old is Anna now?

    _____

Name _____

     Practise Mental Maths 10 – 11 ©A&C Black 2011

Test 39

Warm up

1. What is six twelfths as a percentage?

   _____

2. Write an addition problem where the answer is 1001.

   _____ + _____ = 1001

3. 462 + 96 = ?

   _____

Quick fire

4. What needs to be subtracted from 35621 to make 1219?

   _____

5. What is the total weight of 250g + 900g + 505g + 95g?

   _____

6. 13 × 9 = 90 + (3 × 9) = ? _____

7. 16 × 9 = 90 + (6 × 9) = ? _____

8. 15 × 9 = 90 + (5 × 9) = ? _____

9. 20 × 9 = 90 + (10 × 9) = ? _____

Problem solver

10. The corner shop sells sweets in small bags. Each bag has 12 lemon fizzes. The store sells twice as many chocolate buttons in each bag as lemon fizzes. How many chocolate buttons are there in each bag?

   _____

Name _____

Test 40

Warm up

1. Which is less? 7 thousands or 71 hundreds?

   _____

2. 212 + ? = 326 _____

3. 800 + 390 + 260 = _____

Quick fire

4. Estimate the answer to the nearest 100.

   4143 + 7675 = ?

   _____

5. Which number is exactly halfway between 2413 and 2633?

   _____

6. 117 ÷ 9 = ? _____

7. 144 ÷ 9 = ? _____

8. 135 ÷ 9 = ? _____

9. 180 ÷ 9 = ? _____

Problem solver

10. The tennis team were going to a match. The tennis balls are packed 20 to a box, and they need to take 150 balls. How many boxes do they need to open to have enough balls?

   _____

Name _____

Test 41

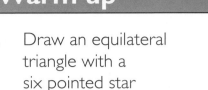

Warm up

1. Double 78.5.

   _____

2. What do I add to 1550 to make 2000?

   _____

3. 137 + 55 + 30 =

   _____

Quick fire

4. What fraction is the shaded part?

   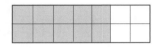 _____

5. Continue this sequence of decimals.

   85.23   85.24 _____ _____ _____

6. 175 + 25 = ? _____

7. 87 + 113 = ? _____

8. 97 + 103 = ? _____

9. 55 + 145 = ? _____

Problem solver

10. A plain cricket sweater costs £29.95. A sweater with a World Cup badge on it costs 3 times as much. How much does the sweater with the badge cost?

    _____

Name _____

Test 42

Warm up

1. Draw an equilateral triangle with a six pointed star inside.

2. Write a number between 2000 and 5000 that is nearer 2000.

   _____

3. 81 ÷ 9 × 3 = _____

Quick fire

4. Count back in steps of 2 from 1001.

   1001 _____ _____ _____ _____

5. Estimate the numbers on this line.

   0 $\quad$ □ $\quad$ □ $\quad$ 1000

6. 179 − 59 = ? _____

7. 187 − 67 = ? _____

8. 169 − 49 = ? _____

9. 171 − 52 = ? _____

Problem solver

10. Kamaljit was in hospital for 220 minutes while his broken arm was put in plaster. How many hours and minutes was he there?

    _____

Name _____

Practise Mental Maths 10 – 11 ©A&C Black 2011

Test 43

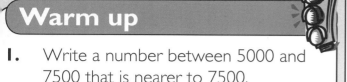

Warm up

1. Write a number between 5000 and 7500 that is nearer to 7500.

   _____

2. Circle the numbers which are not exact multiples of 9.

   27   900   63   98   108

3. Add the digits in today's date.

   _____

Quick fire

4. Round these numbers to the nearest 10.

   94177 12219 13312 78224 1735

   _____ _____ _____ _____ _____

5. Order these numbers, starting with the smallest.

   5012 5630 4929 4006 7325

   _____ _____ _____ _____ _____

6. ____ × ____ = 9

7. ____ × ____ = 72

8. ____ × ____ = 99

9. ____ × ____ = 108

Problem solver

10. $\frac{5}{20}$ of the people on the beach were not sitting under umbrellas. There were 100 people at the beach. How many were sitting under umbrellas?

    _____

Test 44

Warm up

1. Write a subtraction problem where the answer is 1001.

   _____ − _____ = 1001

2. How many minutes are there in 21 hours?

   21 × 60 = _____

3. What is 50% of £4.60? _____

Quick fire

4. Round these fractions to the nearest whole number.

   $116\frac{20}{25}$ _____ $41\frac{17}{20}$ _____ $211\frac{82}{500}$ _____

5. Underline the smaller number in each pair.

   9323 9129   7346 7461

6. 9 ÷ ? = 1 _____

7. 72 ÷ ? = 8 _____

8. 99 ÷ ? = 11 _____

9. 108 ÷ ? = 12 _____

Problem solver

10. Charles is making a chess board. He has a piece of wood 68cm square. He needs to paint 64 squares on his board. How big will each square be?

    _____

---

ame ....

Name ....

Test 45

Warm up

1. Write this number in words: 90101

_____

_____

2. Multiply each of these numbers by 9.

    4   6   9

_____   _____   _____

3. Add the digits in your date of birth and then add 25.

_____

Quick fire

4. Round these decimals to the nearest whole number.

3241.68   4082.731 2211.07 7916.6023

_____   _____   _____   _____

5. Estimate the measures on this line.

36ins   48ins

6. $99 + 99 + 99 = ?$ _____

7. $97 + 93 + 99 = ?$ _____

8. $98 + 93 + 99 = ?$ _____

9. $92 + 98 + 90 = ?$ _____

Problem solver

10. 10,000 ants live in an ants' nest. 76% of them are out hunting. How many are left in the nest?

_____

Test 46

Warm up

1. Circle the number which is half of 7560

3230   873   3780   4230

2. Divide each of these numbers by 8.

   16   32   48

_____   _____   _____

3. What is 75% of 2m?

_____

Quick fire

4. Circle the numbers which are exact multiples of 11.

638   121   4261   10857 89761

5. Circle the larger number in each pair.

48761 47861   19123   11932

6. $102 - 22 - 24 = ?$ _____

7. $114 - 28 - 22 = ?$ _____

8. $106 - 46 - 40 = ?$ _____

9. $110 - 30 - 50 = ?$ _____

Problem solver

10. Imagine a 0–99 number square. Which number is four squares below 51?

_____

Name _____

Name _____

Test 47

Warm up

1. Circle the even numbers.

   1014   1213   1222   1932

2. Choose the correct operation for this calculation.

   $24 \underline{} 6 = 4$

3. How many legs are there on 80 tables?

   _____

Quick fire

4. Circle the numbers which are exactly divisible by 15.

   3000   1050   1300   4500   2750

5. Estimate the numbers on this line.

   1.2   1.4

6. $8 \times 9 = ?$ _____

7. $2 \times 36 = ?$ _____

8. $4 \times 18 = ?$ _____

9. $3 \times 24 = ?$ _____

Problem solver

10. Michelle is 7 years and 5 months old. How old will she be 15 years and 9 months from now?

    _____

Test 48

Warm up

1. What is eight ninths of 90?

   _____

2. $100 - 50 - 74 = ?$ _____

3. What is 10% of 4kg? _____

Quick fire

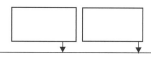

4. Which five coins make £1.55p?

   ___ + ___ + ___ + ___ + ___ = £1.55p

5. Estimate the measures on this line.

   25mm   30mm

6. $72 \div 8 = ?$ _____

7. $72 \div 2 = ?$ _____

8. $72 \div 9 = ?$ _____

9. $72 \div 3 = ?$ _____

Problem solver

10. Sandy is 5 years older than Kajan. 5 years from now, Sandy will be 20. How old is Kajan now?

    _____

Test 49

Warm up

1. What is two eighths as a percentage?

    _____

2. Write a pair of numbers which total 60102.

    _____ + _____ = 60102

3. What is 15% of £60? _____

Quick fire

4. Continue the sequence of 9, starting at 27 and stopping at 90.

    27 ____ ____ ____ ____ ____ ____ 90

5. Order the decimals. Start with the smallest.

    6.55   6.45   6.5   6.08   6.8

    ____ ____ ____ ____ ____

6. 225 + 125 = ? _____

7. 155 + 195 = ? _____

8. 300 + 50 = ? _____

9. 200 + 155 = ? _____

Problem solver

10. If the fire station answers an average of 46 calls every month, how many calls will they answer during a year?

    _____

Name ....

Test 50

Warm up

1. Write a multiplication problem where the answer is 35.

    _____ × _____ = 35

2. 599 + ? = 632 _____

3. Add the digits in today's date and then add your age.

    _____

Quick fire

4. Continue this sequence of fractions.

    $4\frac{3}{10}$ $4\frac{4}{10}$ ____ ____ ____ ____

5. Estimate the times on this line.

    4am _____ 12 noon

6. 300 − 150 = ? _____

7. 295 − 145 = ? _____

8. 250 − 100 = ? _____

9. 255 − 105 = ? _____

Problem solver

10. Each table at the model plane club has space for 4 people to work. How many tables will they need for 38 members to work?

    _____

Name ....

Test 51

Warm up

1. Round 11987 to the nearest 10.

   _____

2. Circle the number which is not an exact multiple of 12.

   48   112   60   24   84

3. How many laces are there in 950 pairs of football boots?

   _____

Quick fire

4. Estimate the answer to the nearest 10

   1919 + 2929 = _____

5. Write this division calculation as a multiplication calculation.

   81 ÷ 9 = 9   _____

6. 9 × 9 = ?   _____

7. 10 × 9 = ?   _____

8. 8 × 9 = ?   _____

9. 11 × 9 = ?   _____

Problem solver

10. Sarah saved £22.12. Then she earned £12.75 for babysitting and £17.95 for picking apples. How much did she have then?

    _____

Test 52

Warm up

1. Write this number in figures:
   Four thousand and twenty six.

   _____

2. Write a pair of numbers which total 6168.

   _____ + _____ = 6168

3. What time would it be 84 minutes before 20:10?

Quick fire

4. Write this addition calculation as a subtraction calculation.

   53 + 48 = 101 _____

5. Find the difference between 7463 and 4998.

   _____

6. _____ ÷ 9 = 9

7. 90 ÷ _____ = 9

8. _____ ÷ 8 = 9

9. 99 ÷ _____ = 9

Problem solver

10. How many hours and minutes are there between 3:46pm on Monday and 8:25pm on Tuesday?

    _____

Test 53

Warm up

1. Round 399999 to the nearest 100.

   _____

2. Write a multiplication problem where the answer is 108.

   _____ × _____ = 108

3. 450 + 17 − 92 = _____

Quick fire

4. Which five coins make £3.20?

   ___ + ___ + ___ + ___ = £3.20

   ____ ____ ____ ____ ____

5. Estimate the numbers on this line.

   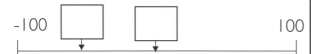

6. 101 + 101 + 103 = ? _____

7. 115 + 95 + 105 = ? _____

8. 115 + 185 + 105 = ? _____

9. 175 + 125 + 95 = ? _____

Problem solver

10. In the Year 6 race, Kate beats Jason's time of 32.6 seconds by 1.9 seconds. What is Kate's time?

    32.6 seconds − 1.9 seconds

    _____

Test 54

Warm up

1. Round 429.76 to the nearest integer or whole number:

   _____

2. Divide each of these numbers by 5.

   50   100   250

   _____ _____ _____

3. What is 75% of 24 hours?

   _____

Quick fire

4. Find the missing numbers.

   _____   9470   _____

   9448   _____

5. Halve these numbers.

   530   984   20861   15009

   ____ ____ ____ ____

6. (305 − 155) − 35 = ? _____

7. (315 − 65) − 65 = ? _____

8. (335 − 35) − 105 = ? _____

9. (345 − 45) − 95 = ? _____

Problem solver

10. Julie bought a piece of fabric 2.75m long for a bedspread. The next week she bought another piece of the same material twice the length to make some curtains. How long was the second piece?

    _____

Name _____   Name _____

Test 55

Warm up

1. What is half of 229.44?

    _____

2. What is the answer to this calculation chain?

    110 − 330 + 550 _____

3. What is 30% of 90? _____

Quick fire

4. What needs to be subtracted from 8212 to make 90?

    _____

5. What is the total weight of

    310g + 1500g + 830g + 155g?

    _____

6. $(2 \times 9) \times 10 = ?$ _____

7. $(7 \times 9) \times 10 = ?$ _____

8. $(9 \times 9) \times 10 = ?$ _____

9. $(6 \times 9) \times 10 = ?$ _____

Problem solver

10. Dionne drank 600ml from a 2L bottle of lemonade. Then her brother drank 700ml. How much lemonade was left?

    _____

Test 56

Warm up

1. What is half of 8050?

    _____

2. $100 − 119 − 20 = ?$

    _____

3. Round 423.55099 to two decimal places.

    _____

Quick fire

4. Double these numbers.

    192   5410   2870   8686

    _____ _____ _____ _____

5. What is the largest number you can make with these digits?

    3   4   0   7   6   4 _____

6. $(180 ÷ 9) ÷ 2 = ?$ _____

7. $(630 ÷ 9) ÷ 7 = ?$ _____

8. $(810 ÷ 9) ÷ 9 = ?$ _____

9. $(540 ÷ 9) ÷ 6 = ?$ _____

Problem solver

10. 200 children go on the school trip. 20% of them bring their mums and there are 20 other adult helpers. How many adults altogether go on the trip?

    _____

Name ....

Name ....

Test 57

Warm up

1. Circle the odd numbers.

   3411   3114   3413   3314

2. Add 19 to each of these numbers.

   19   39   49

   _____   _____   _____

3. $6 \times 8 + 35 =$ _____

Quick fire

4. What needs to be added to change 2028 to 6638?

   _____

5. Which five coins make £3.72p?

   ___ + ___ + ___ + ___ + ___ = £3.72p

6. $100 + 260 = ?$ _____

7. $180 + 180 = ?$ _____

8. $300 + 60 = ?$ _____

9. $140 + 220 = ?$ _____

Problem solver

10. Imagine a 0–99 number square. Which number is eight squares to the right of 71?

   _____

Name ....

Test 58

Warm up

1. Which number is 4002 more than 4020?

   _____

2. $127 + ? = 400$ _____

3. How many minutes are there in 8.30 hours?

   _____

Quick fire

4. Estimate the answer to the nearest 100

   $5050 + 6748 =$

   _____   _____

5. Give the value in £ of

    $\times 65$

   _____

6. $310 - 140 = ?$ _____

7. $340 - 170 = ?$ _____

8. $350 - 180 = ?$ _____

9. $330 - 165 = ?$ _____

Problem solver

10. Calendar Challenge.

   If the 13th of July is a Saturday, what day is the 1st of September?

   _____

Name ....

Practise Mental Maths 10 – 11 ©A&C Black 2011

Test 59

Warm up

1. Write a division problem where the answer is 9.

    _____ ÷ _____ = 9

2. 2020 + 80 + 400 = ? _____

3. What is 20% of 500ml? _____

Quick fire

4. Double these numbers.

    826   3237   9073   8021

    _____ _____ _____ _____

5. Add the decimals

    21.20 + 34.11 + 11.296 = _____

6. ? × 9 = 81 _____

7. ? × 9 = 45 _____

8. ? × 9 = 63 _____

9. ? × 9 = 18 _____

Problem solver

10. In six years Amy will be three times as old as Danny. Danny is four. How old is Amy now?

    _____

Test 60

Warm up

1. How many £5 notes are there in £1760?

    _____

2. What is 40% of 400? _____

3. How many days are there in 7 weeks?

    _____

Quick fire

4. What needs to be subtracted from 7191 to make 4022?

    _____

5. Which number is exactly halfway between 2727 and 3017?

    _____

6. 81 ÷ ? = 9 _____

7. 45 ÷ ? = 5 _____

8. 63 ÷ ? = 7 _____

9. 18 ÷ ? = 2 _____

Problem solver

10. In 8 years Farzana will be 21. She is 2 years older than Denise. How old is Denise now?

    _____

---

ame ....

Test 61

Warm up

1. Double 166.

   _____

2. What do I add to 2222 to make 2800?

   _____

3. 4009 + 120 + 441 = _____

Quick fire

4. What fraction is the shaded part?

   _____

5. Continue this sequence of decimals.

   85.24 85.25 _____ _____ _____

6. 300 + 50 = 250 + ? _____

7. 150 + 200 = 160 + ? _____

8. 290 + 60 = 180 + ? _____

9. 80 + 70 = 110 + ? _____

Problem solver

10. Bobbie is 8 years older than Jhoti. The sum of their ages is 12. How old is Bobbie?

    _____

Name _____

Test 62

Warm up

1. Circle the number which is nearest to 5520.

   5515 5551 5519 5591 5522

2. Write a number between 1500 and 1599 that is nearer 1500.

   _____

3. 650 + 310 + 1000 = _____

Quick fire

4. Count on in steps of 1.25 from 3.

   3 _____ _____ _____ _____

5. Estimate the numbers on this line.

   0 [ ]   [ ]   750

6. (350 − 150) − 50 = ? _____

7. (330 − 180) − 80 = ? _____

8. (310 − 100) − 60 = ? _____

9. (340 − 90) − 50 = ? _____

Problem solver

10. In one term the canteen sold 1476 cartons of orange juice and 2392 cartons of milk. This was half the total of drinks sold in the year. How many cartons of drink were sold in the year?

    _____

Name _____

Test 63

1. Write a number which can be divided by 4 and by 3.
   _____

2. Multiply 15 by 7. _____

3. What is 40% of 5 metres? _____

Quick fire

4. Round these numbers to the nearest 100.

   94171   12213   13312   78224   17351

   _____   _____   _____   _____   _____

5. Order these numbers, starting with the smallest.

   7044   7192   7328   7841   7415

   _____   _____   _____   _____   _____

   Continue the sequences.

6.   2   9   16   ____   ____

7.   11   18   25   ____   ____

8.   17   24   31   ____   ____

9.   29   36   43   ____   ____

Problem solver

10. Mystery numbers.
    If you multiply us and add 5 the answer is 68. Which numbers are we?

    _____

Test 64

Warm up

1. Write the number which is half of 7005.

   _____

2. Write a division problem where the answer is 2.5.

   _____ ÷ _____ = 2.5

3. The circumference of a bean can is 20 of these. Underline the likely measure.

   mm   cm   m

Quick fire

4. Round these fractions to the nearest whole number.

   $21\frac{39}{50}$ _____ $683\frac{16}{20}$ _____ $141\frac{9}{20}$ _____

5. Underline the larger number in each pair.

   21712.12 27121.21   54679.2 56497.2

6. _____ ÷ _____ = 1

7. _____ ÷ _____ = 8

8. _____ ÷ _____ = 11

9. _____ ÷ _____ = 12

Problem solver

10. Jemima's dad is a keen photographer. His collection contains 9597 photos. Albums hold 244 photos. How many albums does he need for his whole collection?

    _____

Name _____

Name _____

Test 65

1. Write this number in words: 99091

   _____

   _____

2. Divide each of these numbers by 15.

   15   75   150

   _____   _____   _____

3. What is 30% of 9kg? _____

Quick fire

4. Round these decimals to the nearest whole number.

   321.419   408.731   221.007   913.602

   _____   _____   _____   _____

5. Estimate the numbers on this line.

   1mg [   ] [   ] 500mg

6. 195 + 180 = ? _____

7. 105 + 275 = ? _____

8. 115 + 265 = ? _____

9. 101 + 279 = ? _____

Problem solver

10. Alexandra wants to buy a ticket for the concert. It costs £32. She has £17.92. How much more money does she need?

    _____

Name _____

Test 66

Warm up

1. Circle the number which is half of 8990

   4445   4495   448

2. Multiply each of these numbers by 9.

   9   8   10   12

   _____ _____ _____ _____

3. 826 + ? = 900   _____

Quick fire

4. Circle the numbers which are exact multiples of 11.

   638   1111   4261   10857   98761

5. Underline the larger number in each pair.

   98799   98778   100321   103021

6. 345 − 90 = ? _____

7. 305 − 50 = ? _____

8. 335 − 80 = ? _____

9. 325 − 60 = ? _____

Problem solver

10. Calendar Challenge.

    What will the date be 3 weeks after December 25th?

    _____

Name _____

Test 67

Warm up

1. Circle the even numbers

 1112   2223   3334   4445

2. What time would it be 32 minutes after 13:30?

3. What is 15% of 500? _____

Quick fire

4. Circle the numbers which are exactly divisible by 8.

 3090   2010   2000   5000   7568

5. Estimate the numbers on this line.

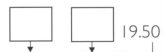

 18.50   [ ]   [ ]   19.50

6. $10 \times 9 = ? \times 2$ _____

7. $4 \times 9 = ? \times 2$ _____

8. $6 \times 9 = ? \times 2$ _____

9. $8 \times 9 = ? \times 2$ _____

Problem solver

10. In the swimming marathon, Sadie beat the school record of 4.69 minutes by 0.23 minutes. What was her time?

_____

Name ....

Test 68

Warm up

1. Which number is 476 less than 1478?

_____

2. Circle the number which is an exact multiple of 25.

 35   65   75   105   145

3. Write an addition problem where the answer is 2176.

 _____ + _____ = 2176

Quick fire

4. Continue this sequence.

 104 111 ____ ____ ____ ____ ____

5. Estimate the measures on this line.

 4mm   [ ]   [ ]   6mm

6. $72 \div 9 = 16 \div ?$ _____

7. $72 \div ? = 24 \div 3$ _____

8. $72 \div 9 = 80 \div ?$ _____

9. $72 \div ? = 56 \div 7$ _____

Problem solver

10. How many pencils are there in 25 packs, if each pack contains 12 pencils?

_____

Name ....

Test 69

1. Which is less? 72 hundreds or 7 thousands?

   _____

2. $(46 + 9) \times 7 = ?$ _____

3. What is 25% of 6 hours? _____

Quick fire

4. Continue the sequence of 7, starting at 77 and stopping at 126.

   77 ____ ____ ____ ____ ____ ____ ____ 126

5. Order decimals. Start with the smallest.

   11.76   11.7   11.26   11.59   11.02

   _____ _____ _____ _____ _____

6. $200 + 200 = 100 + ?$ _____

7. $350 + 50 = 360 + ?$ _____

8. $250 + 150 = 399 + ?$ _____

9. $400 + 0 = 210 + ?$ _____

Problem solver

10. A measuring jug holds 1000 ml. It is about one third full. About how many more ml must I add to fill it?

    _____

Name _____

Test 70

Warm up

1. Round 83666 to the nearest ten.

   _____

2. How many £10 notes are there in £1370?

   _____

3. Write a number which can be divided by 2 and by 6.

   _____

Quick fire

4. Continue the sequence of fractions.

   $112\frac{1}{16}$ $112\frac{2}{16}$ _____ _____ _____ _____

5. Estimate the dates on this line.

   14 Jan [____] [____]   25 Feb

6. $350 - 50 = 345 - ?$ _____

7. $305 - 55 = 345 - ?$ _____

8. $340 - 40 = 345 - ?$ _____

9. $315 - 65 = 345 - ?$ _____

Problem solver

10. Marta made 240 peppermint creams. She coloured 20% green, 30% blue. The rest were white. How many peppermint creams were white?

    _____

Name _____

Test 71

1. Circle the number which is not an exact multiple of 6.

72   150   120   95   66

2. Write a multiplication problem where the answer is 72.

_____ × _____ = 72

3. How many cans of cola are there in 7 six packs?

_____

Quick fire

4. Estimate the answer to the nearest 100.

61912 − 45634 = _____   _____

5. Write this multiplication calculation as a division calculation.

12 × 10 = 120 _____

6. 302 × 2 = ? _____

7. 400 × 2 = ? _____

8. 450 × 2 = ? _____

9. 500 × 2 = ? _____

Problem solver

10. Imagine a 0−99 number square. Which number is five squares above 73?

_____

Test 72

Warm up

1. Write this number in figures: one hundred and eighty one thousand two hundred and ten.

_____

2. Write a pair of numbers which total 799.

_____ + _____ = 799

3. How many minutes are there in $9\frac{3}{4}$ hours?

_____

Quick fire

4. Find the difference between 6924 and 3029. _____

5. Write this addition calculation as a subtraction calculation.

87 + 66 = 153 _____

6. 604 ÷ 2 = ? _____

7. 800 ÷ 2 = ? _____

8. 900 ÷ 2 = ? _____

9. 1000 ÷ 2 = ? _____

Problem solver

10. Calendar Challenge

If the 3rd of June is on a Tuesday, what day is the 1st of July?

_____

Name ....

Name ....

Test 73

Warm up

1. Write a number between 20,000 and 200,000 that is nearer to 20,000.

_____

2. What time is it 84 minutes before 14:56?

3. What is 50% of 500 + 10% of 100?

_____

Quick fire

4. Continue the sequence.

173   281 _____ _____ _____ _____ _____

5. Estimate the numbers on this line.

-11 | |‾‾| |‾‾| -1
    |_____↓_____↓_____|

6. 250 + 250 = ? _____

7. 300 + 200 = ? _____

8. 100 + 400 = ? _____

9. 50 + 450 = ? _____

Problem solver

10. The sum of Don's and Zeta's ages is 19. The product of their ages is 90. Zeta is one year younger. How old is she?

_____

Name _____

Test 74

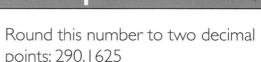

Warm up

1. Round this number to two decimal points: 290.1625

_____

2. Subtract 28 from each of these numbers.

35   42   49

_____   _____   _____

3. How many months are there in 20 years?

_____

Quick fire

4. Find the missing numbers.

5678   3678   _____

_____   _____

5. What are the largest and smallest numbers you can make with these digits? 8 8 7 0 7

Largest _____   Smallest _____

6. 345 – 195 = ? _____

7. 305 – 155 = ? _____

8. 335 – 185 = ? _____

9. 315 – 165 = ? _____

Problem solver

10. There are 476 children in Newbold Middle School and 639 children in Newbold First School. How many children altogether attend the two schools?

_____

Name _____

Test 75

1. What is half of 500.55?

   _____

2. Write a number over 50 which can be divided by 8 and 4.

   _____

3. What is two tenths of 170?

   _____

Quick fire

4. Halve these numbers.

   1010   954   1163   6042

   _____ _____ _____ _____

5. Which five coins make £4.55?

   ____ + ____ + ____ + ____ + ____ = £4.55?

6. $301 \times 2 = ?$ _____

7. $405 \times 2 = ?$ _____

8. $307 \times 2 = ?$ _____

9. $499 \times 2 = ?$ _____

Problem solver

10. Georgina's cycling club covered 21,467 miles last year. This year they rode 6,425 miles further. How many miles did they cycle this year?

    _____

Name ....

Test 76

Warm up

1. Write a number over 30 which can be divided by 7 and 2.

   _____

2. Write a division problem where the answer is 25.

   _____ ÷ _____ = 25

3. Choose the correct operation for this calculation.

   144 ___ 12 = 12

Quick fire

4. Double these numbers.

   357   1615   4427   2788

   _____ _____ _____ _____

5. What is the largest number you can make with these digits?

   0 9 0 3 7 8 0

   _____

6. $602 \div 2 = ?$ _____

7. $810 \div 2 = ?$ _____

8. $307 \div 2 = ?$ _____

9. $499 \div 2 = ?$ _____

Problem solver

10. Mystery numbers.
    If you multiply us and add 9 the answer is 54. Which two numbers are we?

    _____

Name ....

Test 77

Warm up

1. Circle the odd number.

499   796   890   1210

2. Which number is 1001 more than 99?

_____

3. $36 - 100 - 27 = ?$ _____

Quick fire

4. What needs to be subtracted to change 934 to 98?

_____

5. What is the total length of 60mm + 180mm + 460mm + 65mm?

_____

6. $100 + 110 + 120 = ?$ _____

7. $100 + 150 + 170 = ?$ _____

8. $100 + 140 + 100 = ?$ _____

9. $100 + 150 + 140 = ?$ _____

Problem solver

10. If you divide one of us by the other, and subtract 10 the answer will be − 1. Which numbers are we?

_____

Test 78

Warm up

1. Subtract 25 from each of these numbers
575   595   5115

_____ _____ _____

2. $28 \div 7 \times 7 = ?$

_____

3. Add the digits in today's date and add the total number of days in this month

_____

Quick fire

4. Estimate the answer to the nearest whole number.

$47926.3 + 818.52 =$ _____

5. Give the value in £ of

 $\times 1500$ _____

6. $414 - 66 = ? - 18$ _____

7. $420 - 78 = ? - 12$ _____

8. $366 - 18 = ? - 12$ _____

9. $396 - 36 = ? - 30$ _____

Problem solver

10. Irene bought 6 pot plants as leaving presents for the teachers from the whole class. Each plant cost £5.99. How much did the class spend?

_____

Name _____

Name _____

Practise Mental Maths 10 – 11 ©A&C Black 2011

Test 79

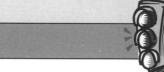

Warm up

1. What number is three eighths of 64?

_____

2. Write a number between 71 and 103 which can be divided by 8 and by 4.

_____

3. How many years are there in 5.5 centuries?

_____

Quick fire

4. Estimate the answer to the nearest 100.

$460 + 794 + 300 =$

_____

5. Add these decimals.

$321.91 + 22.08 + 290.162 =$ _____

6. $(10 \times 9) + (3 \times 9) = ?$ _____

7. $(7 \times 9) + (4 \times 9) = ?$ _____

8. $(8 \times 9) + (1 \times 9) = ?$ _____

9. $(11 \times 9) + (9 \times 9) = ?$ _____

Problem solver

10. Calendar Challenge.
How many months are there between the 1st of January 2001 and the 1st of January 2003?

_____

Name ....

Test 80

Warm up

1. Circle the numbers which are exact multiples of 30.

90   180   150   130   160

2. What time would it be 135 minutes after 23:50?

3. What is 12% of 1 hour? _____

Quick fire

4. Make 477 using four of these numbers.

27   250   200   100   150

____ + ____ + ____ + ____ = 477

5. What number is exactly halfway between 3010 and 3090.

_____

6. $(117 \div 9) \div 13 = ?$ _____

7. $(99 \div 9) \div 11 = ?$ _____

8. $(63 \div 9) \div 7 = ?$ _____

9. $(18 \div 9) \div 2 = ?$ _____

Problem solver

10. Martin, Mel and Mike are a relay team. Martin ran his section of the relay in 10.52 seconds, Mel ran his section in 12.06 seconds and Mike ran his in 12.47 seconds. What was the time for the team?

_____

Name ....

Test 81

Warm up

1. Double 1999.

   _____

2. Write a number between -100 and 100 that is nearer -100.

   _____

3. 570 + 330 + 440 = ? _____

Quick fire

4. What fraction is the shaded part?

   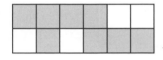

   _____

5. Continue this sequence of decimals.

   -1.05 – 1.06 _____ _____ _____

6. 245 + 255 = ? _____

7. 125 + 375 = ? _____

8. 195 + 305 = ? _____

9. 275 + 225 = ? _____

Problem solver

10. How many biscuits are there in 14 packets if each packet contains 26 biscuits?

    _____

Name _____

Test 82

Warm up

1. Draw a scalene triangle with a circle in it.

2. Write a number between 99 and 125 which can be divided by 20 and 15.

   _____

3. 8 × 8 = ?

   _____

Quick fire

4. Count back in steps of .75 from 6.75.

   6.75 _____ _____ _____ _____

5. Estimate the numbers on this line.

   200 [   ] [   ]   1200

6. 504 – 84 = ? _____

7. 588 – 168 = ? _____

8. 540 – 120 = ? _____

9. 600 – 180 = ? _____

Problem solver

10. Mystery Numbers.
    I am between 80 and 100. When you divide me by six the answer is five more than when you divide me by nine. Which number am I?

    _____

Name _____

Practise Mental Maths 10 – 11 ©A&C Black 2011

Test 83

1. Circle the number which is nearest to 4999.

   5501   4896   4889   5005   5001

2. Write a pair of numbers which total 5,101,010.

   _____ + _____ = 5,101,010

3. 192 + ? = 2500

   _____

Quick fire

4. Round these numbers to the nearest 1000.

   41383   34746   28294   89591   17461

   _____ _____ _____ _____ _____

5. Order these, starting with the largest.

   6309   6571   6031   6013   6124

   _____ _____ _____ _____ _____

6. $(4 \times 9) + (6 \times 9) = ?$ _____

7. $(3 \times 9) + (7 \times 9) = ?$ _____

8. $(9 \times 9) + (1 \times 9) = ?$ _____

9. $(5 \times 9) + (5 \times 9) = ?$ _____

Problem solver

10. Prakesh was carrying a 10L bucket of water. He tripped and spilled 1375ml. How much water was left?

    _____

Test 84

Warm up

1. Round 3461.9650 to one decimal point.

   _____

2. Write a number under 50 which can be divided by 2.5 and 5.

   _____

3. 30 + 820 + 760 =

   _____

Quick fire

4. Round these fractions to the nearest whole number.

   $69\frac{28}{50}$ _____ $41\frac{36}{70}$ _____ $89\frac{15}{17}$ _____

5. Underline the smaller number in each pair.

   2010231 2010321   1270727 1277072

6. $(36 \div 9) \times (54 \div 9) = ?$ _____

7. $(27 \div 9) \times (63 \div 9) = ?$ _____

8. $(81 \div 9) \times (9 \div 9) = ?$ _____

9. $(45 \div 9) \times (45 \div 9) = ?$ _____

Problem solver

10. Shaun, the carpet salesman, cut 3 lengths of 12.5m of carpet from a 58m roll. How much carpet was left on the roll?

    _____

Name ....

Test 85

1. Write this number in words: 81201

   _____

   _____

2. Round 999.998 to the nearest integer or whole number:

   _____

3. Divide each of these numbers by 4.

   8   16   28

   _____   _____   _____

Quick fire

4. Round these decimals to the nearest whole number.

   68.9   700.2   140.9   280.5

   _____   _____   _____   _____

5. Estimate the weights on this line.

   30g [ ] [ ]   90g

6. 400 + 25 = ?   _____

7. 380 + 45 = ?   _____

8. 280 + 145 = ?   _____

9. 345 + 80 = ?   _____

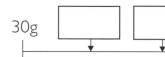
Problem solver

10. On games afternoon there were 220 children at the Sports Hall. 40% of them were wearing shorts. The rest were wearing tracksuits. How many children were wearing tracksuits?

    _____

Name _____

Test 86

Warm up

1. Write a number between 100 and 300 which can be divided by 10 and 50.

   _____

2. What is the answer to this calculation chain?

   48 ÷ 6 × 7 =   _____

3. What is 20% of 400? _____

Quick fire

4. Circle the numbers which are exact multiples of 12.

   50   240   144   670   384

5. Circle the larger number in each pair.

   191050403   191054003

   20202202   20202022

6. (414 − 78) − 66 = ?   _____

7. (420 − 84) − 168 = ?   _____

8. (366 − 72) − 66 = ?   _____

9. (378 − 138) − 78 = ?   _____

Problem solver

10. Imagine a 0 −100 number square. Which two numbers are diagonally to the left of 54?

    _____

Name _____

Test 87

Warm up

1. Circle the number which is half of 9000.

540   4500   540   5400

2. How many minutes are there in 36 hours?

_____

3. Underline the best unit to measure the area of a football pitch.

mm²   cm²   m²   km²

Quick fire

4. Circle the numbers which are exactly divisible by 8.

9191   8896   6464   9064   9108

5. Estimate the numbers on this line.

2000 [ ] [ ] 4000

6. ? × 7 = 49 _____

7. ? × 9 = 81 _____

8. ? × 8 = 64 _____

9. ? × 6 = 36 _____

Problem solver

10. Class 7 goes to the library every two weeks. They went on the 8th of January. On which other dates in January and February did they go to the library?

_____

Name ....

Test 88

Warm up

1. Circle the even numbers.

41102   42101   41202

2. Add 27 to each of these numbers.

70   7   17

_____   _____   _____

3. What is 25% of £6?

_____

Quick fire

4. Continue the sequence.

73 81 89 ____ ____ ____ ____ ____

5. Estimate the measures on this line.

14km [ ] [ ] 37km

6. ? ÷ 7 = 7 _____

7. ? ÷ 9 = 9 _____

8. ? ÷ 8 = 8 _____

9. ? ÷ 6 = 6 _____

Problem solver

10. The greengrocer sold 146.5kg of red peppers, 287kg of green peppers and 219kg of yellow peppers. How many peppers did he sell altogether?

_____

Name ....

Test 89

Warm up

1. Which number is 482 less than 510?

   _____

2. What is 20% of £10? _____

3. What time would it be 1 hour 20 minutes before 12:40?

Quick fire

4. Continue the sequence of 7, starting at 308 and stopping at 357.

   308 ____ ____ ____ ____ ____ ____ 357

5. Order decimals. Start with the largest.

   2.2   2.21   2.82   2.48   2.28

   ____ ____ ____ ____ ____

6. $200 + 100 + 150 = ?$ _____

7. $210 + 200 + 90 = ?$ _____

8. $150 + 150 + 150 = ?$ _____

9. $190 + 210 + 100 = ?$ _____

Problem solver

10. Year 6 collected the following number of sports equipment tokens from cereal packets: 76 in week 1, 94 in week 2, 107 in week 3, 109 in week 4. For every 100 tokens, they receive a free cricket bat. How many bats did they get?

    _____

Name _____

Test 90

Warm up

1. What do I add to 3000 to make 10000?

   _____

2. Write a division problem where the answer is 0.5.

   _____ ÷ _____ = 0.5

3. What is 30% of 9 litres in cl?

   _____

Quick fire

4. Continue this sequence of fractions.

   $2\frac{48}{100}$ $2\frac{49}{100}$ _____ _____ _____ _____

5. Estimate the times on this line.

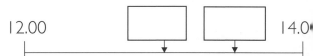

   12.00   14.0

6. $582 - 160 = ?$ _____

7. $510 - 90 = ?$ _____

8. $486 - 66 = ?$ _____

9. $474 - 54 = ?$ _____

Problem solver

10. Dawn's school collected chocolate wrappers for books for the library. They collected 726 in January, 1060 in February and 429 in March. For every 75 tokens, they receive a paperback novel. How many novels did they get?

    _____

Name _____

Test 91

Warm up

1. Round up 542386 to the nearest 100.

   _____

2. Circle the number which is an exact multiple of 14.

   25   13   36   47   52   70

3. Add the digits in today's date and then add 2000.

   _____

Quick fire

4. Which five coins make up £6.40?

   ____ + ____ + ____ + ____ + ____ = £6.40?

5. Write this division calculation as a multiplication calculation.

   $108 \div 9 = 12$ _____

6. $49 =$ ____ $\times$ ____

7. $36 =$ ____ $\times$ ____

8. $81 =$ ____ $\times$ ____

9. $64 =$ ____ $\times$ ____

Problem solver

10. Vandana has 2 litres of milk. How many 125ml milk lollies can she make?

    _____

Test 92

Warm up

1. Write this number in figures: 100,001

   _____

   _____

2. Multiply 18 by 6. _____

3. Write a subtraction problem where the answer is 898.

   _____ − _____ = 898

Quick fire

4. Find the difference between 10204 and 24020?

   _____

5. Complete this addition calculation then write it as a subtraction calculation.

   $492 + 319 =$ ____ _____

6. $49 \div 7 = ?$ _____

7. $36 \div 6 = ?$ _____

8. $81 \div 9 = ?$ _____

9. $64 \div 8 = ?$ _____

Problem solver

10. Mystery numbers.

    If you multiply this number by itself and add 7 the answer is 88. Which number is it?

    _____

---

ame _____   Name _____

Test 93

Warm up

1. Write a number between 300 and 400 which can be divided by 20 and by 40.

   _____

2. Write a division problem where the answer is 250.

   _____ ÷ _____ = 250

3. $880 + ? = 990$

Quick fire

4. Estimate the answer to the nearest 100.

   $5560 + 4470 + 4550 = ?$ _____

5. Estimate the numbers on this line.

   20000 [ ] [ ] 100000

6. $120 + 120 + 120 = ?$ _____

7. $140 + 160 + 200 = ?$ _____

8. $180 + 120 + 160 = ?$ _____

9. $220 + 100 + 140 = ?$ _____

Problem solver

10. Missing number.
    If you divide this number by 12 and add 10 the answer will be 22. What is the missing number?

    _____

Test 94

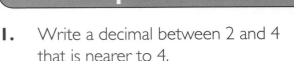

Warm up

1. Write a decimal between 2 and 4 that is nearer to 4.

   _____

2. Subtract 15 from each of these numbers.

   55   60   65

   _____ _____ _____

3. How many sides are there on 90 octagons?

   _____

Quick fire

4. Find the missing numbers.

   _____ _____ _____

   6170   8172

5. What are the largest and smallest numbers you can make with these digits?   0   1   6   3   6

   Largest _____ Smallest _____

6. $(476 - 126) - 70 = ?$ _____

7. $(434 - 77) - 70 = ?$ _____

8. $(469 - 119) - 70 = ?$ _____

9. $(448 - 140) - 70 = ?$ _____

Problem solver

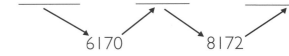

10. Malcolm saved £50.76. He bought a CD for £15.95 and a magazine for £1.25. How much does he have left?

    _____

Name _____

Name _____

Practise Mental Maths 10 – 11 ©A&C Black 2011

Test 95

Warm up

1. What is half of 46665?

_____

2. Choose the correct operation for this calculation.

255 ____ 5 = 51

3. What number is 59 less than 1468?

_____

Quick fire

4. Halve these numbers.

682   1094   93638   42071

_____ _____ _____ _____

5. Order these decimals. Start with the smallest.

52.16   61.9   52.29   51.64   52.02

_____ _____ _____ _____ _____

6. 12 × 10 = ? _____

7. 2 × 60 = ? _____

8. 3 × 40 = ? _____

9. 4 × 30 = ? _____

Problem solver

10. Trains leave for the beach every 50 minutes, starting at 7.30am. Angie arrives at the station at 10.30am. When will the next train leave?

_____

ame ....

Test 96

Warm up

1. What is half of 7007?

_____

2. 4000 − 188 = ? _____

3. How many seconds are there in 2.5 minutes?

_____

Quick fire

4. Halve these numbers.

357   1615   427   278

_____ _____ _____ _____

5. What is the largest number you can make with these digits?

4   0   5   5   3   0

_____

6. 120 ÷ 6 = ? _____

7. 120 ÷ 5 = ? _____

8. 120 ÷ 4 = ? _____

9. 120 ÷ 3 = ? _____

Problem solver

10. Corrine wanted to break her personal record in the 200 metre race. Last year she ran it in 42.36 seconds. This year her time was 37.44 seconds. How much faster did she run this year?

_____

Name ....

Test 97

1. Write an odd number between 206 and 219.

   _____

2. Write an addition problem where the answer is 40401.14.

   _____ + _____ = 40401.14

3. $7 \times 8 + 2000 =$ _____

Quick fire

4. What needs to be subtracted from 9306.25 to make 3193.75?

   _____

5. Give the value in £ of

    × 250

   _____

6. $500 + 10 = ?$ _____

7. $370 + 140 = ?$ _____

8. $255 + 295 = ?$ _____

9. $117 + 393 = ?$ _____

Problem solver

10. Maurice started playing his new computer game at 10.20 am. His mum called him to help her with the lunch at 12.35 pm. How long had he been playing the game?

    _____

Name _____

Test 98

1. Which number is 476 more than 534?

   _____

2. What time would it be 20 minutes after 14:55?

3. What is 10% of £75? _____

Quick fire

4. Estimate the answer to the nearest 100

   $45703 + 82156 + 32417 = ?$ _____

5. What is the total time ?

   40mins + 35mins + 10mins + 10mins?

   _____

6. $640 - 112 = ?$ _____

7. $680 - 152 = ?$ _____

8. $656 - 128 = ?$ _____

9. $648 - 124 = ?$ _____

Problem solver

10. A memory stick holds 1.4 megabytes of information. How many megabytes can be stored on 9 memory sticks?

    _____

Name _____

Practise Mental Maths 10 – 11 ©A&C Black 2011

Test 99

Warm up

1. What percentage of 900 is 72?

_____

2. Multiply each of these numbers by 5.

    10   20   50

_____ _____ _____

3. Underline the best unit to measure the length of a fly's leg.

    cm   mm   m   km

Quick fire

4. What is two fifths of 55?

_____

5. Add these decimals.

$3.45 + 31.33 + 15.07 =$ _____

6. $(6 \times 9) \times 2 = ?$ _____

7. $(7 \times 9) \times 2 = ?$ _____

8. $(4 \times 9) \times 2 = ?$ _____

9. $(5 \times 9) \times 2 = ?$ _____

Problem solver

10. When Primo made some cookies, she used 400ml of milk. Write how much of a litre of milk is left as a decimal.

_____

Test 100

Warm up

1. Which is more? 9 thousands or 98 hundreds?

_____

2. $350 + 280 + 430 = ?$ _____

3. What is 75% of 1 minute? _____

Quick fire

4. Estimate the answer to the nearest 10.

$414141 + 171717$ _____

5. What number is exactly halfway between 3293 and 3403?

_____

6. $(108 \div 9) \div 6 = ?$ _____

7. $(126 \div 9) \div 7 = ?$ _____

8. $(72 \div 9) \div 4 = ?$ _____

9. $(90 \div 9) \div 5 = ?$ _____

Problem solver

10. Manjit bought 5kg of carrots at 28p per kilo and 6kg of pears at 38p per kilo. How much did she spend?

_____

Name ....

Name ....

Test 101

Warm up

1. What do I add to 4500 to make 10000?

   _____

2. Write a negative number between − 4 and − 30 that is nearer − 30.

   _____

3. Circle the number which is not an exact multiple of 110.

   220   303   440   990

Quick fire

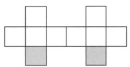

4. What fraction is the shaded part?

       _____

5. Continue this sequence of decimals.

   8.250   8.3   _____ _____ _____

6. 125 + 175 + 145 = ? _____

7. 118 + 112 + 215 = ? _____

8. 135 + 139 + 131 = ? _____

9. 145 + 143 + 147 = ? _____

Problem solver

10. Frank needs 7 pieces of curtain rail, each 35cm long. Curtain rail comes in lengths of 75cm. How many lengths must he buy?

    _____

Name _____

Test 102

Warm up

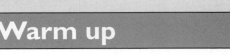

1. Draw an isosceles triangle and mark the two equal angles.

2. 225 ÷ 9 = ? _____

3. Add the digits in today's date and add the number of girls in your class.

   _____

Quick fire

4. Count on in steps of .1 from 7.325

   7.325 _____ _____ _____ _____

5. Estimate the numbers on this line.

   1000   0

6. (584 − 104) − 24 = ? _____

7. (632 − 152) − 40 = ? _____

8. (568 − 8) − 136 = ? _____

9. (600 − 120) − 40 = ? _____

Problem solver

10. Imagine a 0−99 number square. Which number is two squares below and one to the left of 43?

    _____

Name _____

Test 103

Warm up

1. Round 499.890 to one decimal point.

_____

2. Write a multiplication problem where the answer is 84.

_____ × _____ = 84

3. What time would it be 34 minutes after 23:10?

Quick fire

4. Round these numbers to the nearest 1000.

18394   18492   43768   30514   40102

_____ _____ _____ _____ _____

5. Order these numbers, starting with the smallest.

7277   7727   7117   7711   7171

_____ _____ _____ _____ _____

6. $1 \times 9 \times 5 = ?$ _____

7. $10 \times 9 \times 5 = ?$ _____

8. $4 \times 9 \times 5 = ?$ _____

9. $2 \times 9 \times 5 = ?$ _____

Problem solver

10. Imagine a 0–99 number square. Which 2 numbers are diagonally below 88?

_____

Test 104

Warm up

1. Round 999.994 to the nearest integer or whole number.

_____

2. Add 8 to each of these numbers.

14   28   56

_____ _____ _____

3. What is 50% of 1000 litres?

_____

Quick fire

4. Round these fractions to the nearest whole number.

$19\frac{3}{16}$ _____ $29\frac{5}{17}$ _____ $59\frac{8}{12}$ _____

5. Circle the smaller number in each pair.

4141214   4141124

6262362   6262263

6. $(45 \div 9) \div 5 = ?$ _____

7. $(450 \div 9) \div 10 = ?$ _____

8. $(180 \div 9) \div 5 = ?$ _____

9. $(90 \div 9) \div 5 = ?$ _____

Problem solver

10. 430 children want to go to the Summer Playscheme. 240 are girls, the rest are boys. There are only places for 150 boys and 150 girls. How many will be disappointed?

_____

Name _____

Name _____

Test 105

Warm up

1. What is half of 244.85?

_____

2. Multiply each of these numbers by 4.

10   20   30

_____   _____   _____

3. Underline the best measure to find the area of a stamp.

km²   cm²   mm²   m²

Quick fire

4. Round these decimals to the nearest whole number.

1839.05   5160.5   7142.55   4392.75

_____   _____   _____   _____

5. Estimate the numbers on this line.

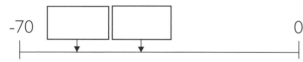

-70 [ ][ ]   0

6. 500 + 80 = ? _____

7. 420 + 160 = ? _____

8. 452 + 128 = ? _____

9. 396 + 184 = ? _____

Problem solver

10. A bag of potatoes weighs 2.75kg. How much do six bags weigh?

_____

Name _____

Test 106

Warm up

1. What is the answer to this calculation chain?

300 + 200 × 4 = _____

2. Write a number between 400 and 700 which can be divided by 25 and by 30.

_____

3. How many days are there in 9 weeks?

_____

Quick fire

4. Circle the numbers which are exact multiples of 8.

4921   7718   9186   448   5232

5. Underline the larger number in each pair.

3003003   3303303

5515521   5575521

6. 640 – 144 = ? _____

7. 592 – 96 = ? _____

8. 624 – 128 = ? _____

9. 576 – 81 = ? _____

Problem solver

10. The netball team practise for 45 minutes on Tuesday, 55 minutes on Wednesday and 1 hour 25 minutes on Friday. How long do they practise each week?

_____

Name _____

Practise Mental Maths 10 – 11 ©A&C Black 2011

Test 107

Warm up

1. Which number is 680 less than 1200?

   _____

2. $524 + ? = 968$

   _____

3. How many wheels are there on 150 tricycles?

   _____

Quick fire

4. Circle the numbers which are exactly divisible by 7.

   1540   6696   4949   2568   7180

5. Estimate the numbers on this line.

   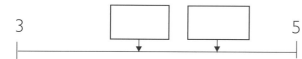

   3   5

6. ____ × ____ = 9

7. ____ × ____ = 16

8. ____ × ____ = 25

9. ____ × ____ = 36

Problem solver

10. During the summer holidays the children's bookshop sold 1628 story books and 2492 non fiction books. How many books did they sell altogether?

    _____

ame ....

Test 108

Warm up

1. Which number is 632 more than 1100?

   _____

2. $(100 - 10) \times 20 = ?$ _____

3. What is 25% of 2 minutes? _____

Quick fire

4. Continue the sequence.

   126   134 ____ ____ ____ ____ ____

5. Estimate the numbers on this line.

   1L   1.5L

6. $9 \div ? = 3$ _____

7. $16 \div ? = 4$ _____

8. $25 \div ? = 5$ _____

9. $36 \div ? = 6$ _____

Problem solver

10. Roy made 3 litres of fruit punch for his group of friends. There were 6 friends in the group. How much fruit punch can each friend drink?

    _____

Name ....

Test 109

1. What number is four sevenths of 49?

_____

2. Write a pair of numbers which total 32201

_____ + _____ = 32201

3. What is 40% of 10kg? _____

Quick fire

4. Continue the sequence of 8, starting at 107 and stopping at 155.

107 ___ ___ ___ ___ ___ ___ 155

5. Order the decimals. Start with the smallest.

0 .1   0 .19   0 .36   0.5   0 .23

___ ___ ___ ___ ___

6. 184 + 116 + 300 = ? _____

7. 198 + 202 + 200= ? _____

8. 168 + 232 + 188 = ? _____

9. 150 + 250 + 188 = ? _____

Problem solver

10. Mystery numbers.
If you multiply us and add 19 the answer is 73. Which two numbers are we?

_____

Name _____

Test 110

Warm up

1. Which is more? 10 thousands or 91 hundreds?

_____

2. 160 + 510 + 190 = ? _____

3. How many months are there in four years?

_____

Quick fire

4. Continue this sequence of fractions.

$\frac{5}{12}$ $\frac{1}{2}$ ___ ___ ___ ___

5. Estimate the times on this line.

17.15 [ ] [ ] 19.45

6. (592 − 32) − 112 = ? _____

7. (576 − 112) − 112 = ? _____

8. (640 − 80) − 112 = ? _____

9. (608 − 48) − 112 = ? _____

Problem solver

10. Missing number.
If you divide this number by 4 and subtract 15 the answer will be − 9. What is the missing number?

_____

Name _____

Test 111

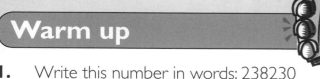
1. Write this number in words: 238230

   _____

   _____

2. How many 20p coins are there in £45?

   _____

3. Circle the number which is an exact multiple of 13.

   92   61   34   26   41

Quick fire

4. Estimate the answer to the nearest 10.

   20204 + 30304 + 40404 = ? _____

5. Write this multiplication calculation as a division calculation.

   25 × 6 = 150 _____

   Continue the sequences.

6. 1   9   17   ____   ____

7. 12   20   28   ____   ____

8. 6   14   22   ____   ____

9. 7   15   23   ____   ____

Problem solver

10. Maryanne bought 5 puzzle books costing £2.95 each. How much did she spend?

    _____

Test 112

Warm up

1. Write this number in figures. One hundred and sixty thousand two hundred and ten.

   _____

2. Multiply 25 by 15. _____

3. What time would it be 36 minutes after 21:36?

Quick fire

4. Make a total of 7001 using four of these numbers.

   254   6000   136   611   1000

   ____ + ____ + ____ + ____ = 7001

5. Write this addition calculation as a subtraction calculation.

   94 + 12 + 11 = 117 _____

6. (81 ÷ 9) ÷ (27÷9) = ? _____

7. (63 ÷ 9) ÷ (7÷1) = ? _____

8. (90 ÷ 9) ÷ (25÷5) = ? _____

9. (54 ÷ 9) ÷ (18÷6) = ? _____

Problem solver

10. Mayling can cycle at 14km per hour. How far will she ride in 6 hours?

    _____

Name ....

Name ....

Test 113

Warm up

1. Circle the number which is nearest to 230.320

    231.320   231.023   230.203

2. Write a number between 100 and 250 that can be divided by 5 and 50.

    _____

3. What is 75% of 4 metres? _____

Quick fire

4. Estimate the answer to the nearest 100

    4142 + 3196 + 7273 = _____

5. Estimate the numbers on this line.

-50   [   ]   [   ]   50

6. 600 + 35 = ? _____

7. 335 + 300 = ? _____

8. 415 + 220 = ? _____

9. 210 + 425 = ? _____

Problem solver

10. It is 3.02km to the library from Norman's house. If Norman visits the library 8 times in one month, how far will he travel?

    _____

Name ....

Test 114

Warm up

1. Round 499.9093 to two decimal places.

    _____

2. Add 40 to each of these numbers.

    60   30   15

    _____ _____ _____

3. How many months are there in a century?

    _____

Quick fire

4. Find the missing numbers.

    39.01   _____   _____

    39.05   39.13

5. What are the largest and smallest numbers you can make with these digits? 8 9 8 5 9

    Largest _____ Smallest _____

6. 631 − 64 = ? _____

7. 583 − 16 = ? _____

8. 615 − 48 = ? _____

9. 599 − 32 = ? _____

Problem solver

10. Nanda ate 0.90 of a bar of chocolate. What fraction of the chocolate bar is left?

    _____

Name ....

Practise Mental Maths 10 – 11 ©A&C Black 2011

Test 115

Warm up

1. What is half of 999?

_____

2. Divide each of these numbers by 4.

      40   80   120

   _____   _____   _____

3. What is 30% of 3m? = ? _____

Quick fire

4. Halve these numbers.

   751   8950   5291   8621

   _____   _____   _____

5. What needs to be subtracted from 8313 to make 4001? _____

6. $18 \times 2 = ? \times 9$ _____

7. $40 \times 2 = ? \times 8$ _____

8. $21 \times 2 = ? \times 7$ _____

9. $24 \times 2 = ? \times 6$ _____

Problem solver

10. At the music store there is a special offer. If you buy a CD you get another at half price. All the CDs are £5.98. Caroline buys 4 CDs. How much does she pay?

_____

Test 116

Warm up

1. Write this number in words: 54007

_____

_____

2. Write four odd numbers between 1200 and 1230.

   _____ _____ _____ _____

3. Choose the correct operation for this calculation.

   $147 \_\_\_\_ 29 = 118$

Quick fire

4. Double these numbers.

   190   4020   538   7863

   _____   _____   _____   _____

5. What is the largest number you can make with these digits?

   1   1   9   1   1   9

                 _____

6. $36 \div 2 = 180 \div ?$ _____

7. $80 \div ? = 64 \div 8$ _____

8. $42 \div ? = 21 \div ?$ _____

9. $48 \div 8 = 54 \div ?$ _____

Problem solver

10. Kenzo spent $\frac{75}{100}$ of his pocket money. He had £5. How much did he spend?

_____

---

ame ....

Name ....

Test 117

Warm up

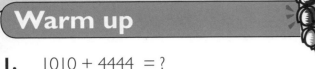

1. $1010 + 4444 = ?$ _____

2. What time would it be 9 minutes after 24:00?

3. $144 \div 12 = ?$ _____

Quick fire

4. What needs to be added to 362.8 to make 956.9?

   _____

5. Make 5020 using four of these numbers.

   2500   2000   520   1500   500

   ___ + ___ + ___ + ___ = 5020

6. $300 + 300 = 400 + ?$ _____

7. $500 + 100 = 250 + ?$ _____

8. $150 + 450 = 110 + ?$ _____

9. $550 + 50 = 195 + ?$ _____

Problem solver

10. Ketan owes his dad £10.25. He earns £3.60 for washing the car, £5.50 for walking Mr Speight's dog, and £2 for mowing the lawn. After he has paid his dad back, how much is left?

    _____

Name ....

Test 118

Warm up

1. Write a multiplication problem where the answer is 90.

   _____ × _____ = 90

2. $100 \times 100 = ?$ _____

3. Write this number 15691. Underline the hundred.

   _____

Quick fire

4. Make 2400 using four of these numbers.

   540   392   99   468   1000

   ___ + ___ + ___ + ___ = 2400

5. Add these decimals.
   $17.47 + 24.31 + 35.5$

   _____

6. $640 - 64 = 592 - ?$ _____

7. $632 - 152 = 640 - ?$ _____

8. $600 - 40 = 640 - ?$ _____

9. $592 - 48 = 560 - ?$ _____

Problem solver

10. Panna is making skipping ropes. Each one must be 1.85m long.
    How many skipping ropes can she cut from 100m of rope?

    _____

Name ....

Test 119

Warm up

1. What number is five sevenths of 49?

_____

2. 429 + ? = 720 _____

3. Total the number of days in June, July and August.

_____

Quick fire

4. Estimate the answer to the nearest whole number.

397.56 + 825.3 = _____   _____

5. Give the value in £ of

 × 1005 _____

6. 502 × 2 = ? _____

7. 600 × 2 = ? _____

8. 550 × 2 = ? _____

9. 504 × 2 = ? _____

Problem solver

10. Bill's watering can holds 5.5 litres. How many times must he fill it to fill his new pond which holds 165 litres?

_____

Test 120

Warm up

1. Which is more? 81 hundreds or 8 thousands?

_____

2. Multiply each of these numbers by 6

9   4   20

_____   _____   _____

3. A bridge measures 0.7 of these. Underline the likely unit of measurement.

km   mm   cm   m

Quick fire

4. Make 8010 using four of these numbers.

4000   976   874   2982   52

____ + ____ + ____ + ____ = 8010

5. What number is exactly halfway between 4324 and 4186?

_____

6. 502 ÷ 2 = ? _____

7. 600 ÷ 2 = ? _____

8. 550 ÷ 2 = ? _____

9. 504 ÷ 2 = ? _____

Problem solver

10. On Thursday the Parmar family drank 2.75L of milk. On Friday they drank 2.25L. On Saturday they drank 3.95L. How much milk did they drink over the three days?

_____

Name _____

Name _____

Test 121

1. Double 170.25.

    _____

2. What do I add to 6900 to make 10000?

    _____

3. Round 314.5557 to one decimal point.

    _____

Quick fire

4. What fraction is the shaded part?

    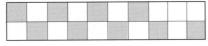   _____

5. Continue this sequence of decimals.

    44.18   44.28   _____   _____   _____

6. 395 + 285 = ?   _____

7. 417 + 263 = ?   _____

8. 119 + 560 = ?   _____

9. 527 + 153 = ?   _____

Problem solver

10. There are 1050kg of nails in the storeroom of Mr Strong's hardware shop. During the week 720kg are sold. How many are left?

    _____

Name _____

Test 122

Warm up

1. Draw a square. Mark the perimeter.

2. Write two numbers between 20 and 50 which are multiples of 7.

    _____

3. What is 75% of one minute?

    _____

Quick fire

4. Count back in steps of .05 from 37.3.

    37.3 _____   _____   _____   _____

5. Estimate the numbers on this line.

6. 632 – 150 = ?   _____

7. 568 – 88 = ?   _____

8. 584 – 104 = ?   _____

9. 616 – 136 = ?   _____

Problem solver

10. Last year a librarian bought 2976 new books. 980 of them were fiction. How many were non fiction?

    _____

Name _____

Test 123

Warm up

1. Write a number between -12 and -20 that is nearer to -12.

   _____

2. Write a pair of numbers which total 7000.

   _____ + _____ = 7000

3. What is 75% of 3 litres? _____

Quick fire

4. Round these numbers to the nearest 100.

   41383   34746   28294   89591   17461

   _____ _____ _____ _____ _____

5. Order these numbers, starting with the largest.

   8031   6824   8301   6240   6420

   _____ _____ _____ _____ _____

6. 501 × 2 = ? _____

7. 515 × 2 = ? _____

8. 601 × 2 = ? _____

9. 616 × 2 = ? _____

Problem solver

10. Tamtown Rovers had a crowd of 1462 at their first match, 978 at their second match and 1213 at their third match. How many spectators did they have altogether?

    _____

Name ....

Test 124

Warm up

1. Round 409.4499 to two decimal points.

   _____

2. Write the number which is half of 3500.

   _____

3. Write a division problem where the answer is 45.

   _____ ÷ _____ = 45

Quick fire

4. Round these fractions to the nearest whole number.

   $361\frac{49}{100}$ $59\frac{26}{30}$ $88\frac{62}{70}$

   _____   _____   _____

5. Underline the smaller number in each pair.

   45545.005   45554.007

   101021.97   101021.96

6. 501 ÷ 2 = ? _____

7. 515 ÷ 2 = ? _____

8. 601 ÷ 2 = ? _____

9. 616 ÷ 2 = ? _____

Problem solver

10. Mystery numbers.
    If you multiply us and subtract 36 the answer is − 4. Which two numbers are we?

    _____

Name ....

Test 125

Warm up

1. Subtract 27 from each of these numbers.

    34   44   97

    _____ _____ _____

2. $976 + ? = 1100$ _____

3. Write a pair of numbers which total 15151.

    _____ + _____ = 15151

Quick fire

4. Round these numbers to two decimal places.

    183.5124 5160.491 7143.876 4392.686

    _____ _____ _____ _____

5. Estimate the weights on this line.

    800g [   ] [   ] 1010g

6. $400 + 300 = 500 + ?$ _____

7. $700 + 0 = ? + 600$ _____

8. $150 + 550 = 650 + ?$ _____

9. $210 + 490 = ? + 610$ _____

Problem solver

10. Missing number.
    If you divide this number by 6 and add 19 the answer will be 26. What is the missing number?

    _____

Name _____

Test 126

Warm up

1. Write the number which is half of 10101.

    _____

2. Multiply each of these numbers by 9.

    3   4   10

    _____ _____ _____

3. What is 75.5% of 100kg?

    _____

Quick fire

4. Circle the numbers which are exact multiples of 15.

    1425   4312   300   96132   7650

5. Circle the larger number in each pair.

    2999.4   2949.9   3155.5   3551.5

6. $586 - 88 = 560 - ?$ _____

7. $608 - 104 = 528 - ?$ _____

8. $584 - 80 = 640 - ?$ _____

9. $576 - 96 = 552 - ?$ _____

Problem solver

10. There are 8 people in Byron's family. His dad takes them all to the Air Show. Tickets are £8.95 each. How much will Byron's dad spend?

    _____

Name _____

Practise Mental Maths 10 – 11 ©A&C Black 2011

Test 127

Warm up

1. Write four even numbers between 1051 and 1071.

   _____ _____ _____ _____

2. $40059 - 49 = ?$

   _____

3. How many milimetres are there in 4 metres?

   _____

Quick fire

4. Circle the numbers which are exactly divisible by 11.

   2531   2310   4620   6619   8547

5. Estimate the numbers on this line.

   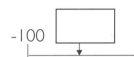

   -100   +500

6. $(2 \times 9) \times (1 \times 10) = ?$ _____

7. $(6 \times 5) \times (1 \times 3) = ?$ _____

8. $(8 \times 5) \times (1 \times 4) = ?$ _____

9. $(7 \times 10) \times (1 \times 5) = ?$ _____

Problem solver

10. Kang can cycle a Kilometre in 4 minutes. How many kilometres could he cycle in 5 hours?

    _____

Test 128

Warm up

1. Which number is 1009 more than 12?

   _____

2. $80800 \div 8 = ?$ _____

3. What will the date be 11 days after the 29th of June?

   _____

Quick fire

4. Continue the sequence.

   1025 1050 _____ _____ _____ _____

5. Estimate the dates on this line.

   1 Feb [   ] [   ]   1 Sept

6. $(90 \div 10) \div 9 = ?$ _____

7. $(180 \div 9) \div 5 = ?$ _____

8. $(160 \div 10) \div 8 = ?$ _____

9. $(350 \div 10) \div 7 = ?$ _____

Problem solver

10. Caitlin practises swimming 3 times a week. The pool is 14.6m long and she swims 15 lengths during each practice session. How far does she swim each week?

    _____

me ....

Name ....

Test 129

1. What percentage of 500 is 125?

    _____

2. Add the digits in today's date and add the number of players in a football team.

    _____

3. Write this number 5761,482 in words. Underline the thousand.

    _____

    _____

Quick fire

4. Continue the sequence of 8, starting at 249 and stopping at 297.

    249____ ____ ____ ____ ____ 297

5. Order these decimals. Start with the smallest.

    58.19   56.19   53.23   51.619   51.85

    ____ ____ ____ ____ ____

6. 700 + 100 = ? _____

7. 350 + 450 = ? _____

8. 298 + 502 = ? _____

9. 396 + 404 = ? _____

Problem solver

10. Jonah earned £20 for helping his mum paint the outside of the house. He spent £5 on a disco ticket, £2.25 on a haircut and £1.20 on a magazine. How much did he have left?

    _____

Name _____

Test 130

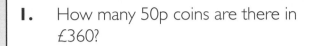

1. How many 50p coins are there in £360?

    _____

2. Write a subtraction problem where the answer is -36.

    _____ – _____ = -36

3. 570 + 90 + 90 = ? _____

Quick fire

4. Continue the sequence of fractions.

    $11\frac{9}{16}$ $11\frac{11}{16}$ ____ ____ ____ ____

5. Estimate the times on this line.

    12:00 [   ] [   ]   24.0

6. ? – 200 = 600 _____

7. ? – 120 = 600 _____

8. ? – 96 = 600 _____

9. ? – 160 = 600 _____

Problem solver

10. A café owner buys drinking straws in packs of 48. How many packs must she buy to get 500 straws? How many will be left over?

    48 into 500 = ? _____

Name _____

Test 131

Warm up

1. Write the word for a period of ten years.

   _____

2. Circle the numbers which are not exact multiples of 10.

   60   81   108   50   110

3. What time would it be 34 minutes after 1:55?

Quick fire

4. Round these numbers to the nearest 1000.

   51263   61679   86291

   _____   _____   _____

5. Write this division calculation as a multiplication calculation.

   600 ÷ 12 = ?   _____

6. (2 × 5) × (7 × 7) = ?   _____

7. (1 × 6) × (5 × 8) = ?   _____

8. (9 × 10)× (1 × 9) = ?   _____

9. (6 × 5) × (3 × 3) = ?   _____

Problem solver

10. Mathias spent 0.95 of his money. What fraction of his money was left?

    _____

Test 132

Warm up

1. Circle the number which is nearest to 31010.

   31007   31012   31015

   31019   31009

2. Multiply 1000 by 12.

   _____

3. What is 10.5% of 200? _____

Quick fire

4. Find the difference between 3368 and 10,000.

   _____

5. Complete this addition calculation and write it as a subtraction calculation.

   112 + 974 = ?   ─   =

   ____ ____ ____ ____

6. (490 ÷ 7) ÷ 7 = ?   _____

7. (240 ÷ 8) ÷ 5 = ?   _____

8. (810 ÷ 9) ÷ 9 = ?   _____

9. (270 ÷ 9) ÷ 5 = ?   _____

Problem solver

10. Phil bought 4kg of strawberries at 92p per kilo and 3kg of cherries at £1.20 per kilo. How much did he spend?

    _____

Name ....

Name ....

Test 133

Warm up

1. Round 1999.999 to the nearest integer or whole number.

   _____

2. Write a subtraction problem where the answer is − 87.

   _____ − _____ = − 87

3. How many mm are there in 5km?

   _____

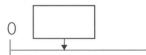

Quick fire

4. Estimate the answer to the nearest 100.

   551150 + 551105 = _____   _____

5. Estimate the numbers on this line.

   0 [☐]   [☐] 10,000

6. 300 + 200 + 110= ? _____

7. 391 + 199 + 113= ? _____

8. 175 + 179 +125= ? _____

9. 450 + 310 + 10= ? _____

Problem solver

10. Over a week the temperatures are 21°, 23°, 21°, 22°, 21°, 23°, 20°. What is the average temperature during the week?

    _____

Name ....

Test 134

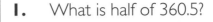

Warm up

1. What is half of 360.5?

   _____

2. For each of these numbers subtract 40.

   55   90   100

   _____   _____   _____

3. Add the days in a leap year February to the number of days in December.

   _____

Quick fire

4. Find the missing numbers.

   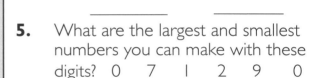

   49236   49368   _____

   _____   _____

5. What are the largest and smallest numbers you can make with these digits?   0   7   1   2   9   0

   Largest _____   Smallest _____

6. (640 −320) − 88 = ? _____

7. (608 −128) − 112 = ? _____

8. (616 − 56) − 136 = ? _____

9. (624 −144) − 144 = ? _____

Problem solver

10. At 1pm there were 9876 people at the theme park. By 4.30pm 1762 people had left and 3216 people had arrived. How many people were in the park at 4.30pm?

    _____

Name ....

Practise Mental Maths 10 – 11 ©A&C Black 2011

Test 135

1. What is half of 4955?

_____

2. What time would it be 11 hours and 3 minutes after 12:19?

3. Divide each of these numbers by 9.

9   81   18

_____ _____ _____

Quick fire

4. Halve these numbers.

7390   1066   4309   6452

_____ _____ _____ _____

5. What needs to be subtracted from 8131 to make 2700?

_____

6. $? \times 4 = 36$ _____

7. $? \times 6 = 54$ _____

8. $? \times 8 = 72$ _____

9. $? \times 9 = 81$ _____

Problem solver

10. In the school 'Charity Maths Challenge' event, Year 5 completed 3271 maths problems and Year 6 maths completed 8263 maths problems. How many maths problems were completed altogether? How much did they raise at 2p per problem?

_____

Test 136

Warm up

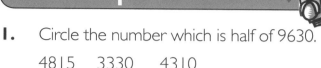

1. Circle the number which is half of 9630.

4815   3330   4310

2. $4 \times 25 \div 20 = ?$ _____

3. Circle the best unit to measure the liquid in a medicine spoon.

cl   pints   ml   litres

Quick fire

4. Halve these numbers.

1900   4020   5318   7864

_____ _____ _____ _____

5. What is the smallest negative number you can make with these digits?

– 5 0 0 2 0 1 0

_____

6. $? \div 4 = 9$ _____

7. $? \div 6 = 9$ _____

8. $? \div 8 = 9$ _____

9. $? \div 9 = 9$ _____

Problem solver

10. Errol's cricket team scored 332 runs in their first innings and 396 runs in their second innings. They beat the other team by 42 runs. What was the other team's score?

_____

Name _____

Test 137

1. Write four odd numbers between 6 and – 12.

   _____

2. Write an addition problem where the answer is 309.5.

   _____ + _____ = 309.5

3. $115 \times 6 = ?$ _____

Quick fire

4. What needs to be added to 2700.9 to make 8131.1?

   _____

5. Add these decimals.

   $107.71 + 20.514 + 360.42 =$ _____

6. $119 + 681 = ?$ _____

7. $217 + 583 = ?$ _____

8. $521 + 279 = ?$ _____

9. $595 + 200 = ?$ _____

Problem solver

10. Mystery numbers.
    If you multiply us and subtract 19 the answer is 9. Which two numbers are we?

    _____

Test 138

Warm up

1. Which number is 154 less than 1279?

   _____

2. Write a number between 80 and 100 which can be divided by 4 and is a double digit.

   _____

3. $1550 + 1750 = ?$ _____

Quick fire

4. Make 5550 using four of these numbers.

   18   3500   568   33   1999

   ____ + ____ + ____ + ____ = 5550

5. Which five coins make £6.40?

   ___ + ___ + ___ + ___ + ___ = £6.40?

6. $624 – 244 = ?$ _____

7. $600 – 220 = ?$ _____

8. $640 – 260 = ?$ _____

9. $632 – 252 = ?$ _____

Problem solver

10. Missing number.
    If you divide this number by 10 and add 27 the answer will be 36. What is the missing number?

    _____

Name _____

Name _____

Practise Mental Maths 10 – 11 ©A&C Black 2011

Test 139

1. What is twelve sixteenths as a percentage?

    _____

2. Subtract 8 from each of these numbers.

        22   36   64

    _____   _____   _____

3. $119 + ? = 190$

    _____

Quick fire

4. Complete the calculation and estimate the answer to the nearest 1000.

    $14960 + 51321 + 41352 = ?$ _____

    _____

5. Round these to two decimal points.

      9.98590   8.9397   3.988

    _____   _____   _____

6. $49 = $ ____ $\times$ ____

7. $90 = $ ____ $\times$ ____

8. $81 = $ ____ $\times$ ____

9. $63 = $ ____ $\times$ ____

Problem solver

10. Sports socks cost £6.80 for 4 pairs. How much does one pair of socks cost?

     _____

Name _____

Test 140

1. Round 12.39887 to the nearest integer or whole number.

     _____

2. Circle the numbers which are exact multiples of 13.

    42   78   52   26   6

3. Circle the best unit to measure the area of the school hall.

    cm^2 km^2 mm^2 m^2

Quick fire

4. Make 4431 using four of these numbers.

    45   2500   237   1661   225

    ____ + ____ + ____ + ____ = 4431

5. What number is exactly halfway between 5162 and 4972?

     _____

6. $49 \div 7 = ?$ _____

7. $90 \div 9 = ?$ _____

8. $81 \div 9 = ?$ _____

9. $63 \div 9 = ?$ _____

Problem solver

10. Alan bought a bunch of flowers. $\frac{2}{6}$ of the flowers were red, $\frac{3}{6}$ were blue and $\frac{1}{6}$ were white. What fraction of the flowers were not white?

     _____

Name _____

Test 141

1. Double 199.75.

   _____

2. Write this number in figures: Forty nine thousand and twenty nine.

   _____

3. How many £20 notes are there in £5000?

   _____

Quick fire

4. What fraction is the shaded part?

   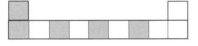 _____

5. Continue this sequence of decimals.

   44.108   44.208 _____ _____ _____

6. $110 + 210 + 190 = ?$ _____

7. $340 + 240 + 80 = ?$ _____

8. $137 + 263 + 139 = ?$ _____

9. $357 + 243 + 97 = ?$ _____

Problem solver

10. Ella is the school champion. She can throw a ball 11,000 cm. How many metres is that?

    _____

Test 142

Warm up

1. Write an odd number between – 25 and – 2.5 that is nearer to – 2.5.

   _____

2. How many £10 notes are there in £5670?

   _____

3. What is the day and date of the fourteenth day after Sunday the 4th of June.

   _____

Quick fire

4. Count back in steps of 900 from 10000.

   10000 _____ _____ _____ _____

5. Estimate the numbers on this line.

   15000   11000

6. $(631 – 71) – 151 = ?$ _____

7. $(567 – 87) – 7 = ?$ _____

8. $(615 – 215) – 67 = ?$ _____

9. $(599 – 119) – 39 = ?$ _____

Problem solver

10. A farmer had 765 potatoes to give away. He shared them equally between 9 bags. How many potatoes were in each bag?

    _____

Name _____

Name _____

Test 143

Warm up

1. Round 8899.9988 to the nearest integer or whole number.

   _____

2. Write a pair of numbers which total 40099.99.

   _____ + _____ = 40099.99

3. How many feet are there in 4 yards?

   _____

Quick fire

4. Round these numbers to the nearest 100.

   40340 71278 65350 52861 69960

   _____ _____ _____ _____ _____

5. Order these numbers, starting with the smallest.

   8301   7999   7450   8239   8235

   ____ ____ ____ ____ ____

6. $11 \times 6 = ?$ _____

7. $11 \times 7 = ?$ _____

8. $11 \times 8 = ?$ _____

9. $11 \times 9 = ?$ _____

Problem solver

10. A packing crate holds six layers of giant chocolate bars with 36 bars in each layer. How many bars are there in 2 crates?

    _____

Name ....

Test 144

Warm up

1. What is half of 5000.1?

   _____

2. Write a subtraction problem where the answer is -299.4

   _____ − _____ = -299.4

3. Circle the best unit to measure the diameter of a pencil?

   m   inches   cm   km   mm

Quick fire

4. Round these fractions to the nearest whole number.

   $119\frac{87}{90}$ _____ $89\frac{46}{80}$ _____ $49\frac{64}{201}$ _____

5. Underline the smaller number in each pair.

   1002003.03   1002003.30

   9499499.49   9499499.94

6. $66 \div 6 = ?$ _____

7. $77 \div 7 = ?$ _____

8. $88 \div 8 = ?$ _____

9. $99 \div 9 = ?$ _____

Problem solver

10. Orla has £23.94. She wants to buy a pair of jeans that cost £42.68. How much more money does she need to save?

    _____

Name ....

Test 145

1. Write 990,200 in words:

   _____

   _____

2. Write a multiplication problem where the answer is 49.7.

   _____ × _____ = 49.7

3. What is nine tenths of 1000?

   _____

Quick fire

4. Round these numbers to one decimal point.

   224.073   772.768   154.584   325.988

   _____   _____   _____   _____

5. Estimate the weights on this line.

   0.5kg [ ] [ ] 1kg

6. 400 + 420 = ? _____

7. 710 + 110 = ? _____

8. 140 + 680 = ? _____

9. 380 + 440 = ? _____

Problem solver

10. If there are 6 red roses in every mixed bunch of 15, how many roses must I buy to get 24 red roses for my mum and dad's wedding anniversary?

    _____

Name _____

Test 146

Warm up

1. Multiply each of these numbers by 7.

   9   12   20

   _____ _____ _____

2. 504 ÷ 9 = ?

   _____

3. It takes 8 of these to drive from London to Edinburgh. Circle the most likely measure.

   minutes   hours   days

Quick fire

4. Circle the numbers which are exact multiples of 6.

   6660   750   751   27072   48961

5. Circle the larger number in each pair.

   3191391   3119319
   7117171   7171171

6. 900 − 160 = ? _____

7. 756 − 18 = ? _____

8. 882 − 144 = ? _____

9. 810 − 72 = ? _____

Problem solver

10. A pack of 20 mixed crayons contains 3 red crayons. How many crayons must Nora the nursery teacher get from the stock room to have 30 red crayons?

    _____

Name _____

Test 147

1. Circle the number which is half of 77.55.

38.750   36.75   38.775

2. Multiply each of these numbers by 5.

2   5   6

_____   _____   _____

3. 1000 + 750 + 440 = ? _____

Quick fire

4. Circle the numbers which are exactly divisible by 25.

2052   2500   2790   2525   2750

5. Estimate the numbers on this line.

450 [ ] [ ] 451

6. 2 × 25 = ? _____

7. 4 × 25 = ? _____

8. 8 × 25 = ? _____

9. 10 × 25 = ? _____

Problem solver

10. Each pack of jelly makes 550ml of jelly. How many litres of jelly will 7 packs make?

_____

Name _____

Test 148

Warm up

1. Write three odd multiples of 7 between 70 and 100.

_____   _____   _____

2. Add 25 to each of these numbers.

11   16   27

_____   _____   _____

3. −426 + 42 = ? _____

Quick fire

4. Continue the sequence

−9 −18 −27 ___ ___ ___ ___ ___

5. Estimate the measures on this line.

20m [ ] [ ] 100m

6. 50 ÷ 25 = ? _____

7. 100 ÷ 25 = ? _____

8. 200 ÷ 25 = ? _____

9. 250 ÷ 25 = ? _____

Problem solver

10. Gareth earned £127.50 cleaning windows for charity. He gave $\frac{2}{5}$ to the Lifeboat charity and the rest to OXFAM. How much money did he give to OXFAM?

_____

Name _____

Test 149

Warm up

1. What is half of 9630?

   _____

2. 7426 + ? = 7816

   _____

3. Write this number. 46606912
   Underline the hundred thousand.

   _____

   _____

Quick fire

4. Continue the sequence of 9, starting at 412 and stopping at 466.

   412 ____ ____ ____ ____ ____ 466

5. Order these decimals. Start with the smallest.
   241.24 214.41 421.14 412.21 214.21

   ____ ____ ____ ____ ____

6. 373 + 373 + 37 = ? _____

7. 411 + 411 + 57 = ? _____

8. 155 + 175 + 317 = ? _____

9. 177 + 373 + 411 = ? _____

Problem solver

10. Patrick collects stamps. He gave 15 of his stamps to Jean, swopped 18 with Megan, then bought a collection of 64. He now has 196 stamps. How many stamps did he have to begin with?

    _____

Name _____

Test 150

Warm up

1. Which is more? 79 hundreds or 846 thousands?

   _____

2. Write three numbers between 210 and 300 which are multiples of 21.

   _____ _____ _____

3. 1478 + 8412 = ? _____

Quick fire

4. Continue this sequence of fractions.

   $-2\frac{3}{8}$ $-2\frac{1}{4}$ _____ _____ _____ _____

5. Estimate the times on this line.

   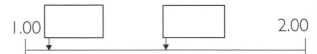

   1.00 [   ]   [   ]   2.00

6. 3 × ? = 21 _____

7. 5 × ? = 45 _____

8. 7 × ? = 56 _____

9. 9 × ? = 81 _____

Problem solver

10. Mystery numbers.
    If you multiply us and subtract 64 the answer is -1. What are the two numbers?

    _____

Name _____

Practise Mental Maths 10 – 11 ©A&C Black 2011

Test 151

Warm up

1. What word do we use for the amount that something can hold?

   _____

2. What time would it be 20 minutes before 00:09?

3. What do I add to 1001 to make 2029?

   _____

Quick fire

4. What needs to be subtracted from 7779 to make -1111?

   _____

5. Complete this multiplication calculation and write it as a division calculation.

   $125 \times 7 = ?$ _____ _____

6. $21 \div ? = 7$ _____

7. $45 \div ? = 9$ _____

8. $56 \div ? = 7$ _____

9. $81 \div ? = 9$ _____

Problem solver

10. Mystery number.
    If you divide this number by 7 and subtract 7 the answer will be 1.

    _____

Test 152

Warm up

1. Draw the cross section of a cylinder.

2. Write a number between 4000 and 4900 that is a multiple of 1500.

   _____

3. Circle the numbers which are exact multiples of 70.

   140   240   136   490

Quick fire

4. Find the difference between 4766.52 and 12792.33.

   _____

5. Complete this addition calculation and write it as a subtraction calculation.

   $999 + \underline{\hspace{1cm}} = 1887$

6. $400 + 500 = ?$ _____

7. $100 + 800 = ?$ _____

8. $120 + 780 = ?$ _____

9. $760 + 140 = ?$ _____

Problem solver

10. A bag of 24 tangerines costs £3.36. How much does one tangerine cost?

    _____

Name ....

Name ....

Test 153

Warm up

1. Circle the number which is nearest to
   - 01010

   -10101   - 01101   - 01011

2. Write a pair of numbers which total 99990.

   _____ + _____ = 99990

3. How many pints are there in 3 gallons?

   _____

Quick fire

4. Continue the sequence

   309   318 ____ ____ ____ ____ ____

5. Estimate the numbers on this line.

   -40 [   ] [   ]   10

6. 873 – 108 = ?_____

7. 783 – 18 = ? _____

8. 801 – 36 = ? _____

9. 837 – 72 = ? _____

Problem solver

10. How many matches are there in 12 boxes if each box contains 48 matches?

    _____

Name _____

Test 154

Warm up

1. Round this number to the nearest hundred: 14949.989

   _____

2. Write a calculation chain where the answer is 1300.

   _____ + _____ = 1300

3. Write the name of the month which comes after the third month of the year.

   _____

Quick fire

4. Find the missing numbers.

   _____   19   _____

               19.25   _____

5. Halve these numbers.

   2944   2227   650   19733

   _____   _____   _____   _____

   Find the missing numbers.

6. 9   18 ____ ____ ____

7. 54 ____ 72 ____ 90

8. 63   72 ____ ____ ____

9. 27 ____ 45 ____ ____

Problem solver

10. At the summer camp there are 500 children. 12 children share each tent. How many tents are needed for all the children?

    _____

Name _____

Test 155

Warm up

1. What is half of 0.5895?

   _____

2. Write a calculation chain where the answer is − 16.

   _____

3. Divide each of these numbers by 12.

   36   96   144

   _____   _____   _____

Quick fire

4. What are the largest and smallest numbers you can make with these digits?   6 2 5 9 8

   Largest _____ Smallest _____

5. Order the decimals. Start with the smallest.

   33.33   33.303   33.133   33.313
   33.113

   _____ _____ _____ _____ _____

6. 999 ÷ 9 = ? _____

7. 306 ÷ 9 = ? _____

8. 270 ÷ 9 = ? _____

9. 540 ÷ 9 = ? _____

Problem solver

10. Damon bought 6kg of potatoes at 60p per kilo and 4kg of cabbage at 92p per kilo. How much did he spend?

    _____

Name ....

Test 156

Warm up

1. Write the number which is half of 0.9999.

   _____

2. Choose the correct operation for this calculation. 480 ___ 8 = 60

3. Write a pair of numbers between 100 and 300 which total 354.

   _____ + _____ = 354

Quick fire

4. Double these numbers.

   2346   2538   3301   5163

   _____ _____ _____ _____

5. What is the smallest negative number you can make with these digits?

   0 1 0 0 1 0 1 0 0 1 −

   _____

6. 300 + 300 + 380 = ? _____

7. 280 + 480 + 180 = ? _____

8. 300 + 100 + 480 = ? _____

9. 180 + 760 + 60 = ? _____

Problem solver

10. Graham's 10.45 bus arrives ten minutes late, and his watch is 20 minutes fast. What time does his watch show when the bus arrives?

    _____

Name ....

Test 157

1. Write three fractions between $\frac{1}{2}$ and $\frac{3}{4}$.

   _____ _____ _____

2. $1456 + 2456 = ?$ _____

3. How many milimetres are there in 2 metres?

   _____

Quick fire

4. What needs to be subtracted from 97625.3 to make 9.4222?

   _____

5. Add these decimals.
   $17.707 + 20.514 + 36.1242 = ?$

   _____

6. $729 - 9 = 900 - ?$ _____

7. $873 - 99 = 864 - ?$ _____

8. $783 - 90 = 873 - ?$ _____

9. $756 - 126 = 810 - ?$ _____

Problem solver

10. Kiri bought a bargain bag of 1500 coloured elastic bands. $\frac{1}{3}$ were red, $\frac{1}{6}$ were blue. How many bands were neither red nor blue?

    _____

Name ....

Test 158

Warm up

1. Which number is 5550 more than 5550?

   _____

2. Write a subtraction calculation where the answer is -94.

   _____ – _____ = -94

3. $9 \times 7 - 60 = ?$ _____

Quick fire

4. Make a total of 4131 using four of these numbers.

   2561   599   111   922   860

   ____ + ____ + ____ + ____ = 4131

5. What is one third of 750? _____

6. $40 \times 2 = 8 \times ?$ _____

7. $45 \times 2 = 10 \times ?$ _____

8. $33 \times 2 = 6 \times ?$ _____

9. $27 \times 2 = 9 \times ?$ _____

Problem solver

10. A strawberry yogurt costs 39p. Mr Day gets 10% off if he buys a tray of 20. How much does he pay for each tray?

    _____

Name ....

Practise Mental Maths 10 – 11 ©A&C Black 2011

Test 159

1. What is nine hundredths as a percentage?

   _____

2. The volume of an egg cup is 50 of these. Circle the most likely measure.

   L   oz   mm   ml   ins

3. $180 \div ? = 12$ _____

Quick fire

4. What needs to be subtracted to change 41414 to -41.414?

   _____

5. Which five coins make 77p?

   ____ + ____ + ____ + ____ + ____ = 77p?

6. $(80 \div 8) \div (80 \div 40) = ?$ _____

7. $(90 \div 9) \div (100 \div 20) = ?$ _____

8. $(99 \div 9) \div (22 \div 2) = ?$ _____

9. $(55 \div 5) \div (9 \div 9) = ?$ _____

Problem solver

10. Over a month, Gopal earned £64.95 for babysitting. He put $\frac{1}{5}$ in the bank and gave $\frac{2}{5}$ to his sister. How much did he have left to spend?

    _____

Test 160

Warm up

1. How many 20p coins are there in £200?

   _____

2. Add 36 to each of these numbers.

   25   50   75

   _____ _____ _____

3. Write this number 8090603. Underline the hundred.

   _____

Quick fire

4. Make 1888 using four of these numbers.

   912   88   696   966   192

   ____ + ____ + ____ + ____ = 1888

5. What number is exactly halfway between 4636 and 5000?

   _____

6. $400 + 591 = ?$ _____

7. $700 + 291 = ?$ _____

8. $351 + 640 = ?$ _____

9. $220 + 771 = ?$ _____

Problem solver

10. Missing number.
    If you divide this number by 9 and add 54 the answer will be 63. What is the missing number?

    _____

Test 161

Warm up

1. Double 45.75.

   _____

2. Write a number between 2000 and 3000 that is exactly divisible by 250.

   _____

3. Circle the numbers which are exact multiples of 88.

   176   353   352   860

Quick fire

4. What fraction is the shaded part?

       _____

5. Continue this sequence of decimals.

   4.18   4.185   _____   _____   _____

6. 900 − 144 = ? _____

7. 783 − 27 = ? _____

8. 946 − 190 = ? _____

9. 937 − 181 = ? _____

Problem solver

10. Iqbal sells peanuts at the zoo. He sold 100 bags on Monday, 140 bags on Tuesday, and then bought 190 more bags on Wednesday. He now has 450 bags of nuts. How many did he have on Monday morning?

    _____

Name _____

Test 162

Warm up

1. Draw a circle. Mark the diameter.

2. Write this number in figures. Seventeen thousand three hundred and forty three.

   _____

3. Write three numbers between 50 and 100 which are not multiples of 7.

   _____ _____ _____

Quick fire

4. Find the difference between 8857 and 8578.

   _____

5. Estimate the numbers on this line.

   -500 [   ]   [   ]   1000

6. $(10 \times 9) = (45 \times 2) = ?$ _____

7. $(3 \times 10) = (15 \times 2) = ?$ _____

8. $(9 \times 8) = (36 \times 2) = ?$ _____

9. $(8 \times 7) = (14 \times 4) = ?$ _____

Problem solver

10. Henry the hippo eats about 25kg of food per day. How much does he weigh if he is about 110 times his daily intake of food?

    _____

Name _____

Test 163

1. Multiply 12 by 9.

   _____

2. 3180 + 1120 + 160 = ? _____

3. How many grammes are there in 45kg?

   _____

Quick fire

4. What are the largest and smallest numbers you can make with these digits? 0 2 0 0 1

   Largest _____ Smallest _____

5. Order these numbers, starting with the largest.
   8762   27680   87026   6287   82607

   _____ _____ _____ _____ _____

6. 800 ÷ 2 = ? _____

7. 810 ÷ 2 = ? _____

8. 900 ÷ 2 = ? _____

9. 1000 ÷ 2 = ? _____

Problem solver

10. Calculators cost £3.25. How much will Mr Smithers have to pay for 7 new calculators for Class 5?

    _____

Test 164

Warm up

1. Write a number between 2000 and 2500 that is exactly divisible by 40.

   _____

2. Write a calculation chain where the answer is -999.

   _____

3. Write the name of the 7th month before the first month of the year.

   _____

Quick fire

4. Find the missing numbers.

5. Circle the smaller number in each pair.

   491949.49   49194.949

   3645972.238   36459722.38

6. 800 + 100 = ? + 200 _____

7. 150 + 755 = ? + 205 _____

8. 450 + 460 = ? + 210 _____

9. 812 + 129 = ? + 240 _____

Problem solver

10. Missing number.
    If you divide this number by 8 and subtract 16 the answer will be − 8. What is the missing number?

    _____

Test 165

1. Write the decimal which is half of 10109.99.

   _____

2. Write a calculation chain where the answer is 1 thousand.

   _____

3. Which is the best unit to weigh a box of apples?

   mg   cl   g   kg   lb

Quick fire

4. Round these decimals to one decimal point.

   1646.446   9657.06   2558.2706   596.705

   _____   _____   _____   _____

5. Estimate the weights on this line.

   1.5g [ ] [ ]   5g

6. 873 − 108 = ? _____

7. 855 − 90 = ? _____

8. 783 − 18 = ? _____

9. 891 − 126 = ? _____

Problem solver

10. Linda bought 8 packs of jelly beans. The beans come in packs of 36. How many beans did she buy?

    _____

Name _____

Test 166

Warm up

1. Write a number which is half a prime number.

   _____

2. For each of these numbers subtract 60.

   65   75   90

   _____   _____   _____

3. Divide each of these numbers by 15.

   45   135   60

   _____   _____   _____

Quick fire

4. Circle the numbers which are exact multiples of 9.

   48369   4698   4608   28191   4662

5. Circle the larger number in each pair.

   110101.10   110100.01

   874784.332   874784.333

6. (7 × 8) × 100 = ? _____

7. (8 × 8) × 100 = ? _____

8. (9 × 9) × 100 = ? _____

9. (9 × 10) × 100 = ? _____

Problem solver

10. A carton of pencils holds 7 layers with 6 boxes in each layer. Each box holds 10 pencils. How many pencils are there in a carton?

    _____

Name _____

Test 167

Warm up

1. Write an even number between 30 and 55 which can be divided exactly by 13.

_____

2. What time would it be 1 hour and a half after 19:19?

3. What is the answer to this calculation chain?

$401 + 194 \div 5 = ?$ _____

Quick fire

4. Circle the numbers which are exactly divisible by 9.

2799   3901   9108   4500   8236

5. Estimate the numbers on this line.

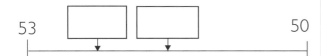

6. $801 \div 2 = ?$ _____

7. $809 \div 2 = ?$ _____

8. $899 \div 2 = ?$ _____

9. $999 \div 2 = ?$ _____

Problem solver

10. Ricky bought 2 pineapples at £2.99 each and 4 grapefruits at 19p each. How much did he spend?

_____

Test 168

Warm up

1. Which number is 1010 less than 1202?

_____

2. Write a multiplication problem where the answer is 380.

_____ × _____ = 380

3. $2120 - 1710 = ?$ _____

Quick fire

4. Continue the sequence.

545   554   563   ____   ____   ____   ____

5. Estimate the measurements on this line.

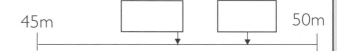

6. $571 + 309 = ?$ _____

7. $131 + 749 = ?$ _____

8. $99 + 681 = ?$ _____

9. $677 + 206 = ?$ _____

Problem solver

10. Keith's watch is 35 minutes slow. His mum says she will meet him in 25 minutes. It is now 3.40pm. What time will Keith's watch show when he meets her?

_____

Test 169

1. Which is more? 540 hundreds or 45 thousands?

   _____

2. 148 ÷ 8 = ? _____

3. Write the name of the 10th month after the second month of the year.

   _____

Quick fire

4. Continue the sequence of 8, starting at 114 and stopping at 162.

   114 ____ ____ ____ ____ ____ 162

5. Order these decimals. Start with the smallest.
   44.888   44.808   44.881   44.188   44.181

   ____ ____ ____ ____ ____

6. 747 − 27 = 900 − ? _____

7. 801 − 171 = 810 − ? _____

8. 900 − 297 = 693 − ? _____

9. 819 − 9 = 900 − ? _____

Problem solver

10. Gloria has used 2.673kg of her 20kg bag of compost to pot up her geraniums. How much does she have left?

    _____

Name _____

Test 170

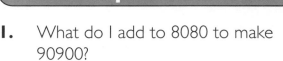

Warm up

1. What do I add to 8080 to make 90900?

   _____

2. Write an addition problem where the answer equals 5 × 20.

   _____ + _____ = _____

3. The height of an eight year old child is 125 of these. Circle the likely measure.

   mm   feet   cm   ins   m

Quick fire

4. Continue this sequence of fractions.

   2   2¼

   ____ ____ ____ ____

5. Estimate the times on this line.

   8.00 [   ] [   ] 14.00

6. 250 × 2 = ? _____

7. 25 × 20 = ? _____

8. 100 × 5 = ? _____

9. 50 × 10 = ? _____

Problem solver

10. Special Offer!
    Marshmallows weigh 128g a packet. In every box of 25 packets there are 3 free packets. What is the total weight of marshmallows in a box?

    _____

Name _____

Test 171

Warm up

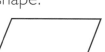

1. Write the name of this shape.

_____

2. -999 + ? = 999 _____

3. Write this number: 1,000,045
Underline the ten.

_____

_____

Quick fire

4. Make 8474 using four of these numbers.

4444   392   444   142   3444

____ + ____ + ____ = 8474

5. Complete this division calculation and write it as a multiplication calculation.

222 ÷ ? = 18.5

_____

6. 810 ÷ 9 ÷ 9 = ? _____

7. 490 ÷ 7 ÷ 7 = ? _____

8. 640 ÷ 8 ÷ 8 = ? _____

9. 500 ÷ 10 ÷ 10 = ? _____

Problem solver

10. Special Offer!
Mountain bike! Was £159.00. Now 12% off. How much does the bike cost now?

_____

Test 172

Warm up

1. Round 82999.9987 to the nearest integer or whole number.

_____

2. Write a pair of numbers which total 1010101.

____ + ____ = 1010101

3. A cheetah can run at a speed of 100 of these. Circle the likely measure.

mph   kph   cmph

Quick fire

4. Find the difference between 857565 and 847464.

_____

5. Complete this addition calculation and write it as a subtraction calculation.

4976 + ? = 8521 _____

6. 350 + 350 = ? + 400 _____

7. 275 + 425 = ? + 100 _____

8. 395 + 305 = ? + 500 _____

9. 324 + 376 = ? + 600 _____

Problem solver

10. Missing number.
If you divide this number by 4 and add 93 the answer will be 100. What is the missing number?

_____

Name _____

Name _____

Test 173

Warm up

1. What is half of 24 × 4? _____

2. Write a multiplication problem where the answer is 4400.

   _____ × _____ = 4400

3. A red kangaroo can spring 10 of these into the air. Circle the likely measurement.

   miles   km   mm   ft   yds

Quick fire

4. What needs to be added to 109109 to make 901901?

   _____

5. Estimate the numbers on this line.

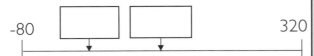

   -80 [ ] [ ]   320

6. (900 − 720) − 90 = ? _____

7. (873 − 153) − 135 = ? _____

8. (792 − 162) − 90 = ? _____

9. (837 − 135) − 162 = ? _____

Problem solver

10. Chirpy Choc Ices cost 43p each. How much will Mrs Singh pay for one each for the 16 children at Jasbir's party?

    _____

Name _____

Test 174

Warm up

1. What is half of 4040.49? _____

2. Add 31 to each of these numbers.

   11   16   27

   _____   _____   _____

3. The KTHI-TV mast in Canada is 629 of these tall. Circle the likely measure:

   cm   mm   ft   m   km   miles

Quick fire

4. Find the missing numbers.

   469.45 _____ _____

         471.5   475.6

5. Halve these numbers.
   10701   13703   40401   90709

   _____ _____ _____ _____

6. 10 × 100 = ? _____

7. 500 × 2 = ? _____

8. 250 × 4 = ? _____

9. 200 × 5 = ? _____

Problem solver

10. Petra cut 10 lengths of 36cm of draught stopper from a 15m roll. How much was left on the roll?

    _____

Name _____

Practise Mental Maths 10 – 11 ©A&C Black 2011

Test 175

Warm up

1. Write three prime numbers between 1 and 20.

   _____ _____ _____

2. Write a number which can be divided by 3, 2, 8, 6 and 4.

   _____

3. Write a calculation chain where the answer is 9.

   _____

Quick fire

4. What needs to be subtracted from 207.33 to make -207.19?

   _____

5. Add these decimals.

   44.66 + 77.77 + 99.11 = _____

6. (190 ÷ 10) ÷ 2 = ? _____

7. (160 ÷ 10) ÷ 3 = ? _____

8. (170 ÷ 10) ÷ 2 = ? _____

9. (180 ÷ 10) ÷ 3 = ? _____

Problem solver

10. 228 children are playing on the field. 50% go in for dinner. Then 50% of those left start playing cricket. How many play cricket?

    _____

Name _____

Test 176

Warm up

1. Subtract 19 from each of these numbers.

   12   18   16

   _____ _____ _____

2. Write two numbers between 50 and 100 which are divisible by 9.

   _____ _____

3. 1130 + 510 + 1110 = ? _____

Quick fire

4. Double these numbers.

   9999   4449   3339   5559

   _____ _____ _____ _____

5. What is the largest number you can make with these digits?
   4 0 0 4 0 4 0 4 0 4

   _____

6. (100 − 80) − 10 = ? _____

7. (97 − 17) − 15 = ? _____

8. (88 − 18) − 10 = ? _____

9. (93 − 15) − 18 = ? _____

Problem solver

10. Special Summer Offer!
    Ice Cream Sundae Spectaculars. Buy 2, get the second at half price. If they normally cost £1.48 each, how much for two at the special offer price?

    _____

Name _____

Test 177

Warm up

1. What percentage of 24 is 8? _____

2. 202020 + 3303030 = ? _____

3. Write this number 4444333.
   Underline the thousands.

   _____

   _____

Quick fire

4. What needs to be added to £515.89
   to make £706.33?

   _____

5. Give the value in £ of

    × 1100 _____

6. 500 + ? = 1000 _____

7. 750 + ? = 1000 _____

8. 680 + ? = 1000 _____

9. 490 + ? = 1000 _____

Problem solver

10. Natasha gets 4 books from the
    library. Each weighs 1.25kg. She also
    has a pencil case weighing 1.05kg and
    a diary weighing 1.75kg. Her bag
    weighs 3.6kg when it is empty. What
    is the weight of her bag with these
    items in it?

    _____

Name ....

Test 178

Warm up

1. Subtract 49 from each of these
   numbers.

   409   499   509

   _____   _____   _____

2. What is the answer to this calculation
   chain?
   566 + 544 × 10 = ? _____

3. How many mm are there in 2m?

   _____

Quick fire

4. What needs to be added to £457.17
   to make £999.11?

   _____

5. Which five coins make 87p?

   ___ + ___ + ___ + ___ + ___ = 87p

6. 1000 − ? = 200 _____

7. 920 − ? = 200 _____

8. 888 − ? = 200 _____

9. 600 − ? = 200 _____

Problem solver

10. Animal Magazine Monthly costs
    £1.15. How many months of the
    magazine can Davy buy for £12?

    _____

Name ....

Practise Mental Maths 10 – 11 ©A&C Black 2011

Test 179

Warm up

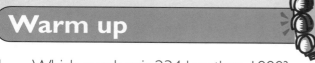

1. Which number is 234 less than 1000?

   _____

2. What do I add to –90 to make 970?

   _____

3. Multiply each of these numbers by 20.

   2   5   7

   _____ _____ _____

Quick fire

4. What are the largest and smallest numbers you can make with these digits? 9 9 0 9 0

   Largest _____ Smallest _____

5. Add these decimals.
   44.777 + 33.888 + 55.999 = ?

   _____

6. $(9 \times 9) \times (2 \times 5) = ?$ _____

7. $(7 \times 7) \times (1 \times 10) = ?$ _____

8. $(8 \times 4) \times (2 \times 10) = ?$ _____

9. $(2 \times 5) \times (5 \times 10) = ?$ _____

Problem solver

10. The garage has 95 tyres. How many cars can have a full set of four new tyres?

    _____

Test 180

Warm up

1. Write a prime number between 10 and 50 that is nearer 50.

   _____

2. $197 \times 1000 = ?$ _____

3. Write the name of the month which is four months after the eighth month of the year.

   _____

Quick fire

4. Make 509011 using four of these numbers.

   9111   399519   100111   270   399419

   ____ + ____ + ____ + ____ = 509011

5. Which number is exactly halfway between 4491 and 5571?

   _____

6. $? \div 9 = \frac{1}{3}$ of 30 _____

7. $? \div 3 = \frac{1}{10}$ of 100 _____

8. $? \div 9 = \frac{1}{3}$ of 24 _____

9. $? \div 8 = \frac{1}{4}$ of 28 _____

Problem solver

10. The corner shop sold 95 copies of the Evening Echo on each day for 6 days. The Echo costs 19p. How much money did they take over the 6 days?

    _____

Name ....

Name ....

Test 181

Warm up

1. Write this number in figures:
   nine thousand and one.

   _____

2. How many 20p coins are there in £700?

   _____

3. A chicken's egg takes about 21 of these to hatch. Underline the likely measure.

   minutes   hours   seconds   days

Quick fire

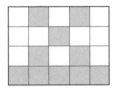

4. What fraction is the shaded part?

   _____

5. Continue this sequence of decimals.

   315.25 315.4 _____   _____   _____

6. $760 + 120 + 100 = ?$ _____

7. $177 + 377 + 411 = ?$ _____

8. $400 + 300 + 281 = ?$ _____

9. $501 + 109 + 209 = ?$ _____

Problem solver

10. To make a cake, you need 250g of margarine. You have 76g in the bowl. How much more do you need?

    _____

Name _____

Test 182

Warm up

1. Draw a pentagon inside a square based pyramid.

2. What do I add to 900 to make 10000?

   _____

3. $144 ÷ ? = 12$ _____

Quick fire

4. Count back in steps of 9 from − 9.

   -9 _____   _____   _____   _____

5. Estimate the numbers on this line.

   100 [____]   [____] 1000

6. $999 − 799 = ?$ _____

7. $889 − 689 = ?$ _____

8. $801 − 601 = ?$ _____

9. $887 − 687 = ?$ _____

Problem solver

10. Missing number.
    If you divide this number by 7 and subtract 20 the answer will be -10. What is the missing number?

    _____

Name _____

Test 183

Warm up

1. Write two prime numbers between 25 and 70.

_____ _____

2. Write a calculation chain where the answer is 0.

_____

3. Which month is 9 months after February?

_____

Quick fire

4. Round these numbers to the nearest 100.

9999   8889   7779   4449   3339

_____ _____ _____ _____ _____

5. Order these, starting with the smallest.

21010   20101   10201   20012   12210

_____ _____ _____ _____ _____

6. $3 \times 4 \times 5 = ?$ _____

7. $4 \times 5 \times 6 = ?$ _____

8. $5 \times 6 \times 7 = ?$ _____

9. $6 \times 7 \times 8 = ?$ _____

Problem solver

10. 4 children each bought roller blades costing £27 a pair. How much did they spend altogether?

_____

Test 184

Warm up

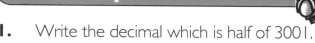

1. Write the decimal which is half of 3001.

_____

2. Write three numbers which end in 8 and are divisible by 8.

_____ _____ _____

3. Multiply 70 by 9

_____

Quick fire

4. Round these fractions to the nearest whole number.

$199 \frac{66}{70}$ _____ $591 \frac{33}{99}$ _____ $889 \frac{14}{25}$ _____

5. Estimate the weights on this line.

1kg |———————[ ]——[ ]———| 10kg

6. $5600 \div 100 \div 8 = ?$ _____

7. $6400 \div 100 \div 8 = ?$ _____

8. $8100 \div 100 \div 9 = ?$ _____

9. $9000 \div 100 \div 9 = ?$ _____

Problem solver

10. Karen buys 12 boxes of strawberries at 30p each and 12 kiwi fruits at 9p each. How much does she spend?

_____

Name ....

Name ....

Test 185

Warm up

I. Write this number in words:
10007000

_____

_____

2. Write a pair of numbers which total the same as 407 − 302.

_____   _____

3. How many corners are there on 70 heptagons?

_____

Quick fire

4. Round these decimals to two decimal points.

111.192   111.912   111.999   111.921

_____   _____   _____   _____

5. Circle the numbers which are exactly divisible by 9.

8981   8991   9000   500   3416

6. 773 + ? = 1000 _____

7. 541 + ? = 1000 _____

8. 377 + ? = 1000 _____

9. 299 + ? = 1001 _____

Problem solver

10. Special Offer!
All CDs £5.99! Buy 5 – only pay for 4. How much does it cost for 5 CDs?

_____

Name _____

Test 186

Warm up

I. What is half of 45 × 6? _____

2. Write a subtraction problem where the answer is -1000.

_____ − _____ = -1000

3. An Olympic athlete can throw a javelin a distance of 90 of these. Circle the likely measure:

mm   miles   cm   feet   m

Quick fire

4. Circle the numbers which are exact multiples of 7.

3500   4492   64   7177   8491

5. Underline the smaller number in each pair.

1101011.101   11001110.101

4424142.660   4421442.660

6. (864 − 144) − 99 = ? _____

7. (855 − 108) − 108 = ? _____

8. (765 − 135) − 126 = ? _____

9. (819 − 99) − 189 = ? _____

Problem solver

10. Gerry collected 2000 cans for charity. The cans were worth 0.05p each. How much did Gerry make for his favourite charity?

_____

Name _____

Practise Mental Maths 10 – 11 ©A&C Black 2011

Test 187

1. Write a fraction which is more than a $\frac{1}{3}$ and less than a $\frac{2}{3}$.

   _____

2. Write a calculation where the answer is a prime number.

   _____

3. $120 \times 6 = ?$ _____

Quick fire

4. Double these numbers.

   110099   44991   88888   99999

   _____ _____ _____ _____

5. What are the largest and smallest decimal numbers you can make with these digits?   2   0   2   0   3   .

   Largest _____ Smallest _____

6. $500 \div ? \div 5 = 10$ _____

7. $500 \div ? \div 5 = 4$ _____

8. $500 \div ? \div 5 = 1$ _____

9. $500 \div ? \div 5 = 2$ _____

Problem solver

10. A farmer's trailer holds 72 bales of hay. There are 1100 bales of hay in his fields. How many trips does Dave need to make to collect all the bales?

    _____

Name ....

Test 188

Warm up

1. Which number is 105.5 less than 200?

   _____

2. Add 155 to each of these numbers.

   17   22   35

   _____ _____ _____

3. Circle the best unit to measure the distance between your eyes.

   cm   km   mm   ins

Quick fire

4. Continue the sequence.

   66 99 ____ ____ ____ ____ ____

5. Estimate the numbers on this line.

   0 [____] [____] | million

6. $400 + 400 + 140 = ?$ _____

7. $503 + 205 + 101 = ?$ _____

8. $120 + 540 + 280 = ?$ _____

9. $309 + 301 + 199 = ?$ _____

Problem solver

10. 9 friends order an extra large pizza to share. The pizza costs £6.30. How much must each friend pay?

    _____

Name ....

Test 189

1. What is four fifteenths of 300?

   _____

2. Multiply each of these numbers by 15.

   2   8   5

   _____ _____ _____

3. What is the answer to this calculation chain?

   2225 + 275 + 45 = ? _____

Quick fire

4. Continue the sequence of 12, starting at 34 and stopping at 118.

   34 ___ ___ ___ ___ ___ ___ 118

5. Order these decimals. Start with the smallest.

   10.101 10.901 10.009 10.900 10.100

   _____ _____ _____ _____ _____

6. 792 – ? = 630 _____

7. 810 – ? = 630 _____

8. 900 – ? = 630 _____

9. 882 – ? = 630 _____

Problem solver

10. Paddy's grandad said he would pay him 5p for every 5 apples he picked. Paddy picked 1790 apples. How much did he earn?

    _____

Test 190

Warm up

1. Which is more? 171 thousands or 4876 hundreds?

   _____

2. What time would it be 80 minutes before 13:07?

3. 4280 + 8240 = ?

   _____

Quick fire

4. Circle the numbers which are exact multiples of 23.

   122   138   3450   345   5966

5. Estimate the months on this line.

   May   [   ]   [   ]   Jan

6. 1000 ÷ ? ÷ 10 = 1 _____

7. 1000 ÷ ? ÷ 5 = 4 _____

8. 1000 ÷ ? ÷ 20 = 2 _____

9. 1000 ÷ ? ÷ 10 = 10 _____

Problem solver

10. The 30 children in Class 6 raised £195 for the school library. Each child raised the same amount. How much did they each raise?

    _____

Name ....

Name ....

Answers for Practise Mental Maths 10 – 11

TEST 1
1. 194
2. 200
3. 1860
4. $\frac{9}{10}$
5. 1300
6. 120
7. 120
8. 120
9. 120
10. 7649

TEST 2
1. (parallelogram)
2. 39
3. 7:55
4. 1400
5. 4876 4902 5794 6381 7002
6. 100
7. 100
8. 100
9. 100
10. 16908

TEST 3
1. 294
2. 4994
3. 67
4. 31000 33000 23000 50000 66000
5. 1325 and 2370
6. 90
7. 108
8. 117
9. 99
10. 11660

TEST 4
1. Accept any correct answer that totals 1000
2. 44 92 200
3. 362
4. 242 18 37
5. 5131 5794
6. 0
7. 2
8. 3
9. 1
10. 188

TEST 5
1. 2280
2. Accept any correct answer that totals 324
3. Answers will vary
4. 502 828 6610 6438
5. Accept any reasonable estimate
6. 316
7. 297
8. 203
9. 181
10. 1310

TEST 6
1. Six thousand, four hundred and sixty
2. 60 70 80
3. 48
4. 200 4488 5552
5. 6829   7011
6. 81
7. 100
8. 9
9. 119
10. 3856

TEST 7
1. 6881
2. 27 18 36
3. 210
4. 1608 1600 1552
5. 4286   3917
6. 45
7. 54
8. 36
9. 63
10. 361

TEST 8
1. 4038
2. 19:26
3. 5p
4. 48 52 56 60 64 68
5. Accept any reasonable estimate
6. 5
7. 6
8. 4
9. 7
10. 2330

TEST 9
1. 18
2. 94
3. 5cm
4. 47 51 55 59 63 67 71
5. .12 .2 .32 .5 .89
6. 160
7. 160
8. 160
9. 160
10. 330

TEST 10
1. 50%
2. Accept any correct answer that totals 18
3. 9:12
4. $35\frac{1}{2}$ 36 $36\frac{1}{2}$ 37
5. Accept any reasonable estimate
6. 70
7. 70
8. 70
9. 70
10. 86

TEST 11
1. Five thousand and twenty one
2. 111
3. 56
4. 30.5 30.6 30.7
5. $3 \times 50 = 150$
6. 4
7. 6
8. 3
9. 10
10. 1461

TEST 12
1. 73512
2. Accept any number above 5250
3. 10
4. $129 - 53 = 76$
5. Accept any reasonable estimate
6. 36
7. 54
8. 27
9. 90
10. 6250kg

TEST 13
1. Accept any number above 3008.5
2. 3000
3. £1
4. 1305 1315
5. Accept any reasonable estimate
6. 240
7. 180
8. 120
9. 144
10. 250

TEST 14
1. 6460
2. 51
3. £6
4. 128 424 600 194
5. 95510 01559
6. 60
7. 44
8. 22
9. 30
10. 9

TEST 15
1. 67
2. 1.1
3. Accept any correct answer that totals 90
4. £1.20
5. 108.95
6. 29 23
7. 26 20 8
8. 27 21 15
9. 28 22 10
10. 1907

TEST 16
1. 2500
2. 60
3. 750
4. 692 1038 1654 1552
5. 1.2478
6. 21
7. 36
8. 56
9. 63
10. 47 and 49

TEST 17
1. 1 5 10
2. –
3. 21:27
4. 2271
5. Accept any reasonable estimate
6. 125
7. 125
8. 125
9. 126
10. 264

TEST 18
1. 844 852
2. Accept any correct answer that totals 2176
3. 14
4. 499
5. 984g
6. 95
7. 95
8. 85
9. 95
10. 21

TEST 19
1. 24
2. 80
3. 180
4. 90 94 98 102 106
5. 1085g
6. Accept any correct answer that totals 54
7. Accept any correct answer that totals 27
8. Accept any correct answer that totals 18
9. 8 and 9
10. £98.03

TEST 20
1. 5 thousands
2. 65 75 90
3. 1860
4. 52 59 66 73 80 87
5. 4870
6. 5
7. 6
8. 7
9. 3
10. 80

TEST 21
1. 252
2. Accept any number below 1550
3. 92
4. $\frac{1}{4}$
5. 48.4 48.5 48.6 48.7
6. 90
7. 40
8. 50
9. 25
10. $\frac{1}{30}$

TEST 22
1.

2. 32 48 88
3. 10
4. 1.5 2 2.5 3
5. Accept any reasonable estimate
6. 100
7. 90
8. 110
9. 15
10. 5298

TEST 23
1. 2461
2. Accept any correct answer that totals 891
3. 112
4. 31000 33000 23000 72000 50000
5. 44902 45794 45876 47002
6. 220
7. 444
8. 500
9. 660
10. 29409

TEST 24
1. 15500
2. 750
3. 35 42 49
4. 12 17 9
5. 9001 8575
6. 110
7. 222
8. 250
9. 325
10. 500

TEST 25
1. 2750
2. 3 5 8
3. 895
4. 1632 6777 4932 7122
5. Accept any reasonable estimate
6. 200
7. 200
8. 200
9. 200
10. 7

TEST 26
1. Eighty thousand three hundred
2. 400
3. 750
4. 5418
5. 9129 7346
6. 80
7. 80
8. 80
9. 80
10. £28.78

TEST 27
1. 3500
2. Accept any correct answer that totals 64
3. 11:20
4. 3636 2424 6060
5. Accept any reasonable estimate
6. 230
7. 422
8. 414
9. 398
10. 38

TEST 28
1. 1226 208
2. 234
3. 250g
4. 130 136 142 148
5. Accept any reasonable estimate
6. 115
7. 211
8. 207
9. 199
10. 270

TEST 29
1. 3420
2. Accept any correct answer that totals 7002
3. 171
4. 181 186 191 196 201 206
5. 5.09 5.3 5.36 5.63 5.9
6. 200
7. 200
8. 200
9. 210
10. 268

TEST 30
1. 12
2. 59 hundreds
3. £2
4. 20 20$\frac{1}{4}$ 20$\frac{1}{2}$ 20$\frac{3}{4}$
5. Accept any reasonable estimate
6. 10
7. 20
8. 40
9. 20
10. 2500

Practise Mental Maths 10 – 11 ©A&C Black 2011

TEST 31

1. 4350
2. 233
3. 750ml
4. 4297
5. $\frac{60}{4} = 15$
6. 54
7. 72
8. 54
9. 72
10. £361.94

TEST 32

1. 462100
2. 26
3. 150
4. 6001
5. 1001,
   1001 − 448 = 553
6. 3
7. 4
8. 4.5
9. 5
10. 9 hours 35 minutes

TEST 33

1. Accept any reasonable estimate above 4200
2. 102
3. 12:17
4. 2012   2112
5. Accept any reasonable estimate
6. 262
7. 266
8. 270
9. 274
10. $\frac{2}{7}$

TEST 34

1. 67
2. 2502.5
3. Accept any correct answer that totals 3156
4. 265   492   1042.5   754.5
5. 87421   12478
6. 120

---

7. 120
8. 120
9. 110
10. 13

TEST 35

1. 5.25
2. Accept any correct answer that totals 63
3. 10   20   30
4. £51
5. 2200g
6. 10 and 7
7. 10 × 9
8. 10 × 9 and 9 × 8
9. 9 and 9
10. 225

TEST 36

11. 3525
2. 75   95   115
3. 5.5
4. 384   574   1712   10820
5. 0.07899
6. 18
7. 9
8. 14
9. 8
10. 56 and 76

TEST 37

1. 113   3413
2. 20   70   55
3. 649
4. 196
5. 1760g
6. 150
7. 40
8. 10
9. 120
10. 39

TEST 38

1. 820
2. 131
3. 1 hour
4. 100
5. 73.22
6. 76

---

7. 80
8. 90
9. 105
10. 9

TEST 39

1. 50%
2. Accept any correct answer that totals 1001
3. 558
4. 34402
5. 1750
6. 117
7. 144
8. 135
9. 180
10. 24

TEST 40

1. 7 thousands
2. 114
3. 1450
4. 11800
5. 2523
6. 13
7. 16
8. 15
9. 20
10. 7.5

TEST 41

1. 157
2. 450
3. 222
4. $\frac{5}{7}$
5. 85.25   85.26   85.27
6. 200
7. 200
8. 200
9. 200
10. £89.85

TEST 42

1.
2. Accept any number below 3500
3. 27

---

4. 999   997   995   993
5. Accept any reasonable estimate
6. 120
7. 120
8. 120
9. 119
10. 3 hours 40 minutes

TEST 43

1. Accept any number above 6250
2. 27   900   63   108
3. Answers will vary
4. 94180   12220   13310   78220   1740
5. 4006   4929   5012   5630   7325
6. Accept any correct answer that totals 9
7. Accept any correct answer that totals 72
8. Accept any correct answer that totals 99
9. Accept any correct answer that totals 108
10. 75

TEST 44

1. Accept any correct answer that totals 1001
2. 1260
3. £2.30
4. 117   42   211
5. 9129   7346
6. 9
7. 9
8. 9
9. 9
10. 8.5

TEST 45

1. Ninety thousand one hundred and one
2. 36   54   81
3. Answers will vary
4. 3242   4083   2211   7917
5. Accept any reasonable estimate
6. 297
7. 289
8. 290
9. 280
10. 2400

TEST 46

1. 3780
2. 2   4   6
3. 1.5m
4. 638   121   10857
5. 48761   19123
6. 56
7. 64
8. 20
9. 30
10. 91

TEST 47

1. 1014   1222   1932
2. ÷
3. 320
4. 3000   1050   4500
5. Accept any reasonable estimate
6. 72
7. 72
8. 72
9. 72
10. 23 and 2 months

TEST 48

1. 80
2. -24
3. 0.4kg
4. 1 × £1, 2 × 20p, 1 × 10p and 1 × 5p
5. Accept any reasonable estimate
6. 9
7. 36
8. 8
9. 24
10. 10

TEST 49

1. 25%
2. Accept any correct answer that totals 60102
3. £9
4. 36 45 54 63 72 81
5. 6.08 6.45 6.5 6.55 6.8
6. 350

7. 350
8. 350
9. 355
10. 552

TEST 50

1. Accept any correct answer that totals 35
2. 33
3. Answers will vary
4. $4\frac{5}{10}$ $4\frac{6}{10}$ $4\frac{7}{10}$ $4\frac{8}{10}$
5. Accept any reasonable estimate
6. 150
7. 150
8. 150
9. 150
10. 9.5

TEST 51

1. 11990
2. 112
3. 1900
4. 4850
5. $9 \times 9 = 81$
6. 81
7. 90
8. 72
9. 99
10. £52.82

TEST 52

1. 4026
2. Accept any correct answer that totals 6168
3. 18:46
4. $101 - 48 = 53$
5. 2465
6. 81
7. 10
8. 72
9. 11
10. 28 hours and 29 minutes

TEST 53

1. 400000
2. Accept any correct answer that totals 108
3. 375
4. 3 × £1 and 2 × 10p
5. Accept any reasonable estimate

6. 305
7. 315
8. 405
9. 395
10. 30.7 seconds

TEST 54

1. 430
2. 10   20   50
3. 18
4. 9426   9492   9514
5. 265   492   10430.5   7504.5
6. 115
7. 185
8. 195
9. 205
10. 5.5m

TEST 55

1. 114.72
2. 330
3. 27
4. 8122
5. 2795g
6. 180
7. 630
8. 810
9. 540
10. 700ml

TEST 56

1. 4025
2. -39
3. 423.55
4. 384 10820 5740 17372
5. 764430
6. 10
7. 10
8. 10
9. 10
10. 60

TEST 57

1. 3411   3413
2. 38   58   68
3. 83
4. 4610

5. 1 × £2, 1 × £1, 1 × 50p, 1 × 20p and 1 × 2p
6. 360
7. 360
8. 360
9. 360
10. 79

TEST 58

1. 8022
2. 273
3. 510
4. 11800
5. £13
6. 170
7. 170
8. 170
9. 165
10. Sunday

TEST 59

1. Accept any correct answer that totals 9
2. 2500
3. 100ml
4. 1652 6474 18146 16042
5. 66.606
6. 9
7. 5
8. 7
9. 2
10. 24

TEST 60

1. 352
2. 160
3. 49
4. 3169
5. 2872
6. 9
7. 9
8. 9
9. 9
10. 11

TEST 61

1. 332
2. 578
3. 4570
4. $\frac{11}{16}$
5. 85.26 85.27 85.28
6. 100
7. 190

170
40
. 4

EST 62
1. 5519
2. Accept any number below 1549.5
3. 1960
4. 4.25   5.5   6.75   8
5. Accept any reasonable estimate
6. 150
7. 70
8. 150
9. 200
. 7736

EST 63
1. Accept any number that can be divided by 3 and 4
2. 105
3. 2 metres
4. 94200   12200   13300   78200   17400
5. 7044   7192   7328   7415   7841
6. 23 30
7. 32 39
8. 38 45
9. 50 57
. 7 and 9

EST 64
1. 3502.5
2. Accept any correct answer that totals 2.5 cm
3. 22   684   141   27121.21   56497.2
4. Accept any correct answer that totals 1
5. Accept any correct answer that totals 8
6. Accept any correct answer that totals 11
7. Accept any correct answer that totals 12
. 40

EST 65
1. Ninety nine thousand and ninety one

---

2. 1   5   10
3. 2.7kg
4. 321   409   221   914
5. Accept any reasonable estimate
6. 375
7. 380
8. 380
9. 380
10. £14.08

TEST 66
1. 4495
2. 81   72   90   108
3. 74
4. 638   1111   10857
5. 98799   103021
6. 255
7. 255
8. 255
9. 265
10. January 15th

TEST 67
1. 1112   3334
2. 14:02
3. 75
4. 2000   5000   7568
5. Accept any reasonable estimate
6. 45
7. 18
8. 27
9. 36
10. 4.46 minutes

TEST 68
1. 1002
2. 75
3. Accept any correct answer that totals 2176
4. 118   125   132   139   146
5. Accept any reasonable estimate
6. 2
7. 9
8. 10
9. 9
10. 300

TEST 69
1. 7 thousands
2. 385
3. 1.5
4. 84   91   98   105   112   119
5. 11.02   11.26   11.59   11.7   11.76
6. 300
7. 40
8. 1
9. 190
10. 667ml

TEST 70
1. 83670
2. 137
3. Accept any correct number divisible by 2 and 6
4. $112\frac{3}{16}$ $112\frac{4}{16}$ $112\frac{5}{16}$ $112\frac{6}{16}$
5. Accept any reasonable estimate
6. 45
7. 95
8. 45
9. 95
10. 120

TEST 71
1. 95
2. Accept any correct answer that totals 72
3. 42
4. 16300
5. 120 / 10 = 12
6. 604
7. 800
8. 900
9. 1000
10. 23

TEST 72
1. 181210
2. Accept any correct answer that totals 799
3. 585
4. 3895
5. 153 − 66 = 87
6. 302

---

7. 400
8. 450
9. 500
10. Tuesday

TEST 73
1. Accept any number below 110000
2. 13:32
3. 255
4. 389   497   605   713   821
5. Accept any reasonable estimate
6. 500
7. 500
8. 500
9. 500
10. 9

TEST 74
1. 290.16
2. 7   14   21
3. 240
4. 4678   2678   1678
5. 88770   07788
6. 150
7. 150
8. 150
9. 150
10. 1115

TEST 75
1. 250.275
2. Accept any correct number above 50
3. 34
4. 505   477   581.5   3021
5. 1 × £2, 2 × £1, 1 × 50p and 1 × 5p
6. 602
7. 810
8. 614
9. 998
10. 27892

TEST 76
1. Accept any correct number above 30
2. Accept any correct answer that totals 25
3. ÷
4. 714   3230   8854   5576
5. 9873000

6. 301
7. 405
8. 153.5
9. 249.5
10. 5 and 9

TEST 77
1. 499
2. 1100
3. -91
4. 836
5. 765mm
6. 330
7. 420
8. 340
9. 390
10. 9 / 1

TEST 78
1. 550 570 5090
2. 28
3. Answers will vary
4. 48745
5. £150
6. 366
7. 354
8. 360
9. 390
10. £35.94

TEST 79
1. 24
2. Accept any correct number between 71 and 103
3. 550
4. 1600
5. 634.152
6. 117
7. 99
8. 81
9. 180
10. 24

TEST 80
1. 90 150 180
2. 02:05
3. 7.2 minutes

4. 27 + 200 + 100 + 150
5. 3050
6. 1
7. 1
8. 1
9. 1
10. 35.05 seconds

TEST 81
1. 3998
2. Accept any correct number below 0
3. 1340
4. $\frac{2}{3}$
5. -1.07 -1.08 -1.09
6. 500
7. 500
8. 500
9. 500
10. 364

TEST 82
1.

2. Accept any correct number between 99 and 125
3. 64
4. 6 5.25 4.5 3.75
5. Accept any reasonable estimate
6. 420
7. 420
8. 420
9. 420
10. 90

TEST 83
1. 5001
2. Accept any correct answer that totals 5,101,010
3. 2308
4. 41000 35000 28000 90000 17000
5. 6571 6309 6124 6031 6013
6. 90
7. 90

8. 90
9. 90
10. 8625ml

TEST 84
1. 3462.0
2. Accept any correct number below 50
3. 1610
4. 70 42 90
5. 2010231 1270727
6. 24
7. 21
8. 9
9. 25
10. 20.5m

TEST 85
1. Eighty one thousand two hundred and one
2. 1000
3. 2 4 7
4. 69 700 141 281
5. Accept any reasonable estimate
6. 425
7. 425
8. 425
9. 425
10. 132

TEST 86
1. Accept any correct number between 100 and 300
2. 56
3. 80
4. 240 144 384
5. 191054003 20202202
6. 270
7. 168
8. 228
9. 162
10. 43 and 63

TEST 87
1. 4500
2. 2160
3. m²
4. 8896 6464 9064

5. Accept any reasonable estimate
6. 7
7. 9
8. 8
9. 6
10. 22 January, 5 February and 19 February

TEST 88
1. 41102 41202
2. 97 34 44
3. 1.5
4. 97 105 113 121
5. Accept any reasonable estimate
6. 49
7. 81
8. 64
9. 36
10. 652.5kg

TEST 89
1. 28
2. £2
3. 11:20
4. 315 322 329 336 343 350
5. 2.82 2.48 2.28 2.21
6. 450
7. 500
8. 450
9. 500
10. 3

TEST 90
1. 7000
2. Accept any correct answer that totals 0.5
3. 270cl
4. $2\frac{50}{100}$ $2\frac{51}{100}$ $2\frac{52}{100}$ $2\frac{53}{100}$
5. Accept any reasonable estimate
6. 422
7. 420
8. 420
9. 420
10. 29

TEST 91

1. 542400
2. 70
3. Answers will vary
4. 3 × £2 and 2 × 20p
5. 12 × 9 = 108
6. 7 × 7
7. 6 × 6
8. 9 × 9
9. 8 × 8
10. 16

EST 92

1. 100001
2. 108
3. Accept any correct answer that totals 898
4. 13816
5. 811,
6. 811 − 319 = 492
7. 7
8. 6
9. 9
10. 8
11. 9

EST 93

1. Accept any correct number between 300 and 400
2. Accept any correct answer that totals 250
3. 110
4. 14600
5. Accept any reasonable estimate
6. 360
7. 500
8. 460
9. 460
10. 144

EST 94

1. Accept any number above 3
2. 40   45   50

3. 720
4. 5169   7171   9173
5. 66310   01366
6. 280
7. 287
8. 280
9. 238
10. £33.56

TEST 95

1. 23332.5
2. ÷
3. 1409
4. 341   547   46819   21035.5
5. 51.64   52.02   52.16   52.29   61.9
6. 120
7. 120
8. 120
9. 120
10. 11am

TEST 96

1. 3503.5
2. 3812
3. 150
4. 178.5   807.5   213.5   139
5. 554300
6. 20
7. 24
8. 30
9. 40
10. 4.92 seconds

TEST 97

1. Accept any odd numbers between 206 and 219
2. Accept any correct answer that totals 40401.14
3. 2056
4. 6112.5
5. £12.50
6. 510
7. 510
8. 550
9. 510
10. 2 hours and 15 minutes

TEST 98

1. 1010
2. 15:15
3. £7.50
4. 160300
5. 95 minutes
6. 528
7. 528
8. 528
9. 524
10. 12.6

TEST 99

1. 8%
2. 50   100   250
3. mm
4. 22
5. 49.85
6. 108
7. 126
8. 72
9. 90
10. 0.6L

TEST 100

1. 98 hundreds
2. 1060
3. 45 seconds
4. 585860
5. 3348
6. 2
7. 2
8. 2
9. 2
10. £3.68

TEST 101

1. 5500
2. Accept any correct number below -17
3. 303
4. $\frac{1}{5}$
5. 8.35   8.4   8.45
6. 445
7. 445
8. 405
9. 435
10. 4

TEST 102

1.
2. 25
3. Answers will vary
4. 7.425   7.525   7.625   7.725
5. Accept any reasonable estimate
6. 456
7. 440
8. 424
9. 440
10. 62

TEST 103

1. 499.9
2. Accept any correct answer that totals 84
3. 23:44
4. 18000   18000   44000   31000   40000
5. 7117   7171   7277   7711   7727
6. 45
7. 450
8. 180
9. 90
10. 97 and 99

TEST 104

1. 1000
2. 22   36   64
3. 500 litres
4. 19   29   60
5. 4141124   6262263
6. 1
7. 5
8. 4
9. 2
10. 130

TEST 105

1. 122.425
2. 40   80   120
3. mm^2
4. 1839   5161   7143   4393
5. Accept any reasonable estimate

6. 580
7. 580
8. 580
9. 580
10. 16.5kg

TEST 106
1. 2000
2. Accept any correct number between 400 and 700
3. 63
4. 448   5232
5. 3303303   5575521
6. 496
7. 496
8. 496
9. 495
10. 185 minutes

TEST 107
1. 520
2. 444
3. 450
4. 1540   4949
5. Accept any reasonable estimate
6. 1 × 9
7. Accept any correct answer that totals 16
8. Accept any correct answer that totals 25
9. Accept any correct answer that totals 36
10. 4120

TEST 108
1. 1732
2. 1800
3. 30 seconds
4. 142   150   158   166   174
5. Accept any reasonable estimate
6. 3
7. 4
8. 5
9. 6
10. 0.5 litre

TEST 109
1. 28

2. Accept any correct answer that totals 32201
3. 4kg
4. 115   123   131   139   147
5. .1   .19   .23   .36   .5
6. 600
7. 600
8. 588
9. 588
10. 6 and 9

TEST 110
1. 10 thousands
2. 860
3. 48
4. $\frac{7}{12}$ $\frac{2}{3}$ $\frac{9}{12}$ $\frac{5}{6}$
5. Accept any reasonable estimate
6. 448
7. 352
8. 448
9. 448
10. 24

TEST 111
1. Two hundred and thirty eight thousand, two hundred and thirty
2. 225
3. 26
4. 90910
5. 150 / 6 = 25
6. 25 33
7. 36 44
8. 30 38
9. 31 39
10. £14.75

TEST 112
1. 160210
2. 375
3. 22:12
4. 254 + 6000 + 136 + 611
5. 117 − 11 − 12 = 94
6. 3

7. 1
8. 2
9. 2
10. 84km

TEST 113
1. 230.203
2. Accept any correct number between 100 and 250
3. 3 metres
4. 14600
5. Accept any reasonable estimate
6. 635
7. 635
8. 635
9. 635
10. 48.32km

TEST 114
1. 499.91
2. 100   70   55
3. 1200
4. 39.09   39.17
5. 99885   58899
6. 567
7. 567
8. 567
9. 567
10. $\frac{1}{10}$

TEST 115
1. 499.5
2. 10   20   30
3. 0.9m
4. 375.5   4475   2645.5   4310.5
5. 4312
6. 4
7. 10
8. 6
9. 8
10. £17.94

TEST 116
1. Fifty four thousand and seven

2. Accept all odd numbers between 1200 and 1230
3. −
4. 380   8040   1076   157
5. 991111
6. 10
7. 10
8. 7
9. 9
10. £3.75

TEST 117
1. 5454
2. 00:09
3. 12
4. 594.1
5. 2500 + 520 + 1500 + 5
6. 200
7. 350
8. 490
9. 405
10. 85p

TEST 118
1. Accept any correct answer that totals 90
2. 10000
3. Fifteen thousand six hundred and ninety one 15691
4. 540 + 392 + 468 + 100
5. 77.28
6. 16
7. 160
8. 80
9. 16
10. 54

TEST 119
1. 35
2. 291
3. 92
4. 1223
5. £20.10
6. 1004
7. 1200
8. 1100
9. 1008
10. 30

TEST 120
1. 81 hundreds
2. 54   24   120
3. km
4. 4000 + 976 + 2982 + 52
5. 4255
6. 251
7. 300
8. 275
9. 202
10. 8.95L

TEST 121
1. 340.5
2. 3100
3. 314.6
4. $\frac{9}{20}$
5. 44.38   44.48   44.58
6. 680
7. 680
8. 679
9. 680
10. 330kg

TEST 122
1.
2. Accept any correct number between 20 and 50
3. 45 seconds
4. 37.25 37.2 37.15 37.1
5. Accept any reasonable estimate
6. 482
7. 480
8. 480
9. 480
10. 1996

TEST 123
1. Accept any correct number above -16
2. Accept any correct answer that totals 7000
3. 2.25 litres
4. 41400 34800 28300 89600 17500

5. 8301 8031 6824 6420 6240
6. 1002
7. 1030
8. 1202
9. 1232
10. 3653

TEST 124
1. 409.45
2. 1750
3. Accept any correct answer that totals 45
4. 361   60   89
5. 45545.005 101021.96
6. 250.5
7. 257.5
8. 300.5
9. 308
10. 4 and 8

TEST 125
1. 7   17   70
2. 124
3. Accept any correct answer that totals 15151
4. 183.51 5160.49 7143.88 4392.69
5. Accept any reasonable estimate
6. 200
7. 100
8. 50
9. 90
10. 42

TEST 126
1. 5050.5
2. 27   36   90
3. 75.5kg
4. 1425 300 7650
5. 2999.4   3551.5
6. 62
7. 24
8. 136
9. 72
10. £71.60

TEST 127
1. Accept any even numbers between 1051 and 1071
2. 40010
3. 4000
4. 2310 4620 8547
5. Accept any reasonable estimate
6. 180
7. 90
8. 160
9. 350
10. 75

TEST 128
1. 1021
2. 10100
3. 10 July
4. 1075 1100 1125 1150
5. Accept any reasonable estimate
6. 1
7. 4
8. 2
9. 5
10. 657m

TEST 129
1. 25%
2. Answers will vary
3. Five million, <u>seven hundred and sixty one thousand</u>, four hundred and eighty two, 5,7<u>6</u>1,482
4. 257 265 273 281 289
5. 51.619   51.85   53.23   56.19   58.19
6. 800
7. 800
8. 800
9. 800
10. £11.55

TEST 130
1. 720
2. Accept any correct answer that totals -36
3. 750

4. $11\frac{13}{16}$ $11\frac{15}{16}$ $11\frac{1}{16}$ $11\frac{3}{16}$
5. Accept any reasonable estimate
6. 800
7. 720
8. 696
9. 760
10. 10 packs, 4 straws left over

TEST 131
1. Decade
2. 81 108
3. 2:29
4. 51000   62000   86000
5. $50 \times 12 = 600$
6. 490
7. 240
8. 810
9. 270
10. $\frac{5}{100}$

TEST 132
1. 31009
2. 12000
3. 21
4. 6632
5. 1086, 1086 − 974 = 112
6. 10
7. 6
8. 10
9. 6
10. £7.28

TEST 133
1. 2000
2. Accept any correct answer that totals -87
3. 5000000
4. 1102300
5. Accept any reasonable estimate
6. 610
7. 703
8. 479
9. 770
10. 22°

TEST 134
1. 180.25
2. 15   50   60
3. 60
4. 49302   49434   49500
5. 972100   001279
6. 232
7. 368
8. 424
9. 336
10. 11330

TEST 135
1. 2477.5
2. 23:22
3. 1   9   2
4. 3695   533   2154.5   3226
5. 5431
6. 9
7. 9
8. 9
9. 9
10. 11534, £230.68

TEST 136
1. 4815
2. 5
3. ml
4. 950   2010   2659   3932
5. -0000125
6. 36
7. 54
8. 72
9. 81
10. 686

TEST 137
1. Accept any odd numbers between 6 and -12
2. Accept any correct answer that totals 309.5
3. 690
4. 5430.2
5. 488.644
6. 800
7. 800
8. 800
9. 795
10. 7 and 4

TEST 138
1. 1125
2. 88
3. 3300
4. 18 + 3500 + 33 + 1999
5. 3 × £2 and 2 × 20p
6. 380
7. 380
8. 380
9. 380
10. 90

TEST 139
1. 75%
2. 14   28   56
3. 71
4. 108000
5. 9.99   8.94   3.99
6. Accept any correct answer that totals 49
7. Accept any correct answer that totals 90
8. Accept any correct answer that totals 81
9. Accept any correct answer that totals 63
10. £1.70

TEST 140
1. 12
2. 78   52   26
3. m^2
4. 45 + 2500 + 1661 + 225
5. 5067
6. 7
7. 10
8. 9
9. 7
10. $\frac{5}{6}$

TEST 141
1. 399.5
2. 49029
3. 250
4. $\frac{5}{11}$
5. 44.308   44.408   44.508
6. 510
7. 660
8. 539
9. 697
10. 110

TEST 142
1. Accept an odd number above -13.75
2. 567
3. Sunday 18 June
4. 9100   8200   7300   6400
5. Accept any reasonable estimate
6. 409
7. 473
8. 333
9. 441
10. 85

TEST 143
1. 8900
2. .Accept any correct answer that totals 40099.99
3. 12
4. 40300   71300   65400   52900   70000
5. 7450   7999   8235   8239   8301
6. 66
7. 77
8. 88
9. 99
10. 432

TEST 144
1. 2500.05
2. Accept any correct answer that totals -299.4
3. mm
4. 120   90   49
5. 1002003.03   9499499.49
6. 11
7. 11
8. 11
9. 11
10. £18.74

TEST 145
1. Nine hundred and ninety thousand two hundred
2. Accept any correct answer that totals 49.7
3. 900
4. 224.1   772.8   154.6   326.0
5. Accept any reasonable estimate
6. 820
7. 820
8. 820
9. 820
10. 60

TEST 146
1. 63   84   140
2. 56
3. Hours
4. 6660   750   27072
5. 3191391   7171171
6. 740
7. 738
8. 738
9. 738
10. 200 crayons

TEST 147
1. 38.775
2. 10   25   30
3. 2190
4. 2500 2525 110
5. Accept any reasonable estimate
6. 50
7. 100
8. 200
9. 250
10. 3.85 litres

TEST 148
1. Accept any odd multiples of 7 between 70 and 100
2. 36   41   52
3. -384
4. -36   -45   -54   -63   -7
5. Accept any reasonable estimate
6. 2
7. 4
8. 8
9. 10
10. £76.50

TEST 149

1. 4815
2. 390
3. Forty six million, six hundred and six thousand, nine hundred and twelve, 46,<u>6</u>06,912
4. 421 430 439 448 457
5. 214.21 214.41 241.24 412.21 421.14
6. 783
7. 879
8. 647
9. 961
10. 147

TEST 150

1. 846 thousands
2. Accept any correct number between 210 and 300
3. 9890
4. $-2\frac{1}{8}$ -2 $-1\frac{7}{8}$ $-1\frac{3}{4}$
5. Accept any reasonable estimate
6. 7
7. 9
8. 8
9. 9
10. 7 and 9

TEST 151

1. Quantity
2. 23:49
3. 1028
4. 8890
5. 875, 875 ÷ 7 = 125
6. 3
7. 5
8. 8
9. 9
10. 56

TEST 152

1.
   4500

3. 140   490
4. 8025.81
5. 888, 1887 − 888 = 999
6. 900
7. 900
8. 900
9. 900
10. 14p

TEST 153

1. -01011
2. Accept any correct answer that totals 99990
3. 24
4. 327 336 345 354 363
5. Accept any reasonable estimate
6. 765
7. 765
8. 765
9. 765
10. 576

TEST 154

1. 14950
2. Accept any correct answer that totals 1300
3. April
4. 19.5   18.75   18.5
5. 1472   1113.5   325   9866.5
6. 27   36   45
7. 63 81
8. 81   90   99
9. 36   54   63
10. 42

TEST 155

1. 0.29475
2. Accept any correct answer that totals -16
3. 3   8   12
4. 98652   25689
5. 33.113 33.133 33.303 33.313 33.33
6. 111
7. 34
8. 30
9. 60
10. £7.28

TEST 156

1. 0.49995
2. ÷
3. Accept any correct numbers between 100 and 300
4. 4692 5076 6602 10326
5. -0000001111
6. 980
7. 940
8. 880
9. 1000
10. 11:15

TEST 157

1. Accept any correct answer between ½ and ¾
2. 3912
3. 2000
4. 97615.8778
5. 74.3452
6. 180
7. 90
8. 180
9. 180
10. 750

TEST 158

1. 11100
2. Accept any correct answer that totals -94
3. 3
4. 2561 + 599 + 111 + 860
5. 250
6. 10
7. 9
8. 11
9. 6
10. £7.02

TEST 159

1. 9%
2. ml
3. 15
4. 41455.414
5. 1 x 50p, 2 x 10p, 1 x 5p and 1 x 2p

6. 5
7. 2
8. 1
9. 11
10. £25.98

TEST 160

1. 1000
2. 61   86   111
3. Eight million, ninety thousand, six hundred and three, 8,090,<u>6</u>03
4. 912 + 88 + 696 + 192
5. 4818
6. 991
7. 991
8. 991
9. 991
10. 81

TEST 161

1. 91.5
2. Accept any correct number between 2000 and 3000
3. 176   352
4. $\frac{6}{11}$
5. 4.19   4.195   4.2 4.205
6. 756
7. 756
8. 756
9. 756
10. 500

TEST 162

1. (circle diagram)
2. 17343
3. Accept any correct number between 50 and 100
4. 279
5. Accept any reasonable estimate
6. 90
7. 30
8. 72
9. 56
10. 2750kg

TEST 163
1. 108
2. 4460
3. 4500
4. 21000   00012
5. 87026 82607 27680
   8762 6287
6. 400
7. 405
8. 450
9. 500
10. £22.75

TEST 164
1. Accept any correct number between 2000 and 2500
2. Accept any correct answer that totals -999
3. June
4. -140   -187
5. 49194.949 3645972.238
6. 700
7. 700
8. 700
9. 701
10. 64

TEST 165
1. 5054.995
2. Accept any correct answer that totals 1000
3. kg
4. 1646.5   9657.1
   2558.3   596.7
5. Accept any reasonable estimate
6. 765
7. 765
8. 765
9. 765
10. 288

TEST 166
1. Accept any correct number
2. 5   15   30
3. 3   9   4
4. 4698 4608 4662
5. 110101.10   874784.333
6. 5600

---

7. 6400
8. 8100
9. 9000
10. 420

TEST 167
1. Accept any correct number between 30 and 55
2. 20:49
3. 119
4. 2799 9108 4500
5. Accept any reasonable estimate
6. 400.5
7. 404.5
8. 449.5
9. 499.5
10. £6.74

TEST 168
1. 192
2. Accept any correct answer that totals 380
3. 410
4. 572   581   590   599
5. Accept any reasonable estimate
6. 880
7. 880
8. 780
9. 883
10. 3:30pm

TEST 169
1. 540 hundreds
2. 18.5
3. December
4. 122 130 138 146 154
5. 44.181 44.188
   44.808 44.881 44.888
6. 180
7. 180
8. 90
9. 90
10. 17.327kg

TEST 170
1. 82820
2. Accept any correct answer that totals 100
3. cm
4. $2\frac{1}{2}$, $2\frac{3}{4}$, 3, $3\frac{1}{4}$
5. Accept any reasonable estimate
6. 500
7. 500
8. 500
9. 500
10. 3584g

TEST 171
1. Parallelogram
2. 1998
3. One million and forty five, 1,000,0<u>4</u>5
4. 4444 + 444 + 142 + 3444
5. 12, 18.5 × 12 = 222
6. 10
7. 10
8. 10
9. 5
10. £139.92

TEST 172
1. 83000
2. Accept any correct answer that totals 1010101
3. mph
4. 10101
5. 3545,
   8521 − 3545 = 4976
6. 300
7. 600
8. 200
9. 100
10. 28

TEST 173
1. 48
2. Accept any correct answer that totals 4400
3. ft

---

4. 792792
5. Accept any reasonable estimate
6. 90
7. 585
8. 540
9. 540
10. £6.88

TEST 174
1. 2020.245
2. 42   47   58
3. m
4. 473.55 477.65
5. 5350.5 6851.5
   20200.5 45354.5
6. 1000
7. 1000
8. 1000
9. 1000
10. 11.4m

TEST 175
1. Accept any correct number
2. Accept any correct number
3. Accept any correct answer that totals 9
4. 414.52
5. 221.54
6. 9.5
7. 5.3
8. 8.5
9. 6
10. 57

TEST 176
1. -7   -1   -3
2. Accept any correct number between 50 ar 100
3. 2750
4. 19998 8898 6678 11118
5. 4444400000
6. 10
7. 65
8. 60
9. 60
10. £2.22

TEST 177
1. 30%

Practise Mental Maths 10 – 11 ©A&C Black 2011

3505050

Four million, four hundred and <u>forty four</u> thousand, three hundred and thirty three 4,4<u>44</u>333

190.44

£550

500

250

320

510

11.4kg

EST 178

360   450   460

11100

2000

541.94

1 × 50p, 1 × 20p, 1 × 10p, 1 × 5p and 1 × 2p

800

720

688

400

10

EST 179

766

1060

40   100   140

99900   00999

134.664

810

490

640

500

23

EST 180

Accept any correct number above 30

197000

December

9111 + 399519 + 100111 + 270

5031

90

30

72

56

£108.30

TEST 181

1.   9001

2.   3500

3.   Days

4. $\frac{1}{2}$

5.   315.55   315.7   315.85

6.   980

7.   965

8.   981

9.   819

10. 174g

TEST 182

1.

2.   9100

3.   12

4.   -18   -27   -36   -45

5.   Accept any reasonable estimate

6.   200

7.   200

8.   200

9.   200

10. 70

TEST 183

1.   Accept any correct number between 25 and 70

2.   Accept any correct answer that totals 0

3.   November

4.   10000   8900   7800   4400   3300

5.   10201   12210   20012   20101   21010

6.   60

7.   120

8.   210

9.   336

10. £108

TEST 184

1.   1500.5

2.   Accept any correct numbers ending in, and divisible by, 8

3.   630

4.   200   591   890

5.   Accept any reasonable estimate

6.   7

7.   8

8.   9

9.   10

10. £4.68

TEST 185

1.   One hundred thousand seven hundred

2.   Accept any correct answer that totals 105

3.   490

4.   111.19   111.91   112.00   111.92

5.   8991   9000

6.   227

7.   459

8.   623

9.   702

10. £23.96

TEST 186

1.   135

2.   Accept any correct answer that totals -9000

3.   m

4.   3500   8491

5.   11001110.101   4421442.660

6.   621

7.   639

8.   504

9.   531

10. £100

TEST 187

1.   Accept any correct answer between $\frac{1}{3}$ and $\frac{2}{3}$

2.   Accept any correct answer that is a prime number

3.   720

4.   220198   89982   177776   199998

5.   3.2200   0.0223

6.   10

7.   25

8.   100

9.   50

10. 16

TEST 188

1.   94.5

2.   172   177   190

3.   cm

4.   132   165   198   231   264   297

5.   Accept any reasonable estimate

6.   940

7.   809

8.   940

9.   809

10. 70p

TEST 189

1.   80

2.   30   120   75

3.   2545

4.   46   58   70 82   94 106

5.   10.009   10.100   10.101   10.900   10.901

6.   162

7.   180

8.   270

9.   252

10. £1.79

TEST 190

1.   4876 hundreds

2.   11:47

3.   12520

4.   138   3450   345

5.   Accept any reasonable estimate

6.   100

7.   50

8.   25

9.   10

10. £6.50